SECRETS TO EXCEPTIONAL LIVING

TRANSFORMING YOUR LIFE THROUGH THE FRUIT OF THE SPIRIT

by
Joyce Meyer

WARNER FAITH

WARNER BOOKS

An AOL Time Warner Company

Warner Books Edition
Copyright © 2002 by Joyce Meyer
Life In The Word, Inc., P.O. Box 655, Fenton, Missouri 63026
All rights reserved.

Warner Books, Inc., 1271 Avenue of the Americas, New York, NY 10020
Visit our Web site at www.twbookmark.com.

 An AOL Time Warner Company

Printed in the United States of America

ISBN: 0-446-53201-0
LCCN: 2002110827

CONTENTS

INTRODUCTION:

A MORE EXCELLENT WAY OF LIVING

God has made available to us the means for leading an effective, fulfilling, powerful and rewarding life. Preparing ourselves by gaining the knowledge and training we need to live the way we desire will help us, of course. But leading a truly exceptional life beyond imagination comes from recognizing and focusing on what is important in life. And God tells us what is important in His Word.

It is important to God that we develop the qualities of His nature — that we have more love, joy and peace in our lives; more patience, kindness and goodness; more faithfulness, gentleness and self-control — qualities that the Bible calls the fruit of the Spirit.[1] These qualities of God's Spirit are already inside those of us in whom His Spirit lives, those of us who have accepted Jesus Christ as the only acceptable sacrifice for our sins, who have repented of our sins and received Jesus as our personal Savior.

As Christians, many of us pray that God will move powerfully through us to help others, and God wants us to pray this way. He has made available to us *special endowments of supernatural energy* that the Bible also calls *spiritual gifts*[2] to use for that very purpose.[3] But I believe our first **priority** should be developing the fruit of the Spirit.

During the first few years of my ministry, I spent a lot of my prayer time asking God for those special endowments of supernatural energy to operate through me. I thought to be a powerful minister, I would need them. And I do. We all need them. But I didn't give much thought to the fruit of the Spirit. Then one day the Lord impressed upon me, "Joyce, if you would have put even one half of the amount of energy and time into praying about and trying to develop the fruit of the Spirit as you have the gifts, you'd already have both."

The same Scripture passages that tell us to earnestly desire spiritual gifts,[4] especially the greater gifts, also tell us there is a still more excellent way.[5] That more excellent way is love.[6] The following verse shows us an example of how the gifts and love work together.

> *And when Jesus went out He saw a great multitude; and He was moved with compassion for them, and healed their sick.*
> MATTHEW 14:14 NKJV

One of the *special endowments of supernatural energy* that God has made available for us to use is the gifts of healings.[7] In the example above, we see first in Jesus the fruit of the Spirit "love" in the form of compassion, before we see Him move in a gift of the Spirit "healings." First we see the fruit, then the gift. The *more excellent way* "love" is **the** fruit of the Spirit. Love is the fruit from which all the other fruit issue.[8] If God's love is the basis for our actions, we are representing Him well because God **is** love.[9]

Jesus said: . . . *the tree is known and recognized and judged by its fruit.*[10] A good tree can be recognized by its fruit, and that applies to us as much as it does to trees. We are known by our fruit,[11] not by our gifts. We are known to be Jesus' followers by our love for one another,[12] and by our fruit Jesus is known. A display of the fruit of the Spirit, the nature of God, is a display of the character of Jesus Christ. According to 2 Corinthians 5:20 we are God's ambassadors, and He is making His appeal to mankind through us as believers in Jesus Christ. This is a very big responsibility that we should take seriously.

> IF GOD'S LOVE IS THE BASIS FOR OUR ACTIONS, WE ARE REPRESENTING HIM WELL BECAUSE GOD IS LOVE.

As an example of how we can affect another's life through the simplicity of the fruit of the Spirit, I want to quote the words on a card Dave and I received today.

Dear Joyce and Dave,

Words can't begin to express the blessing you have brought to me through God. I was always stressed out, worrying about little things and taking God for granted. Your books, tapes, and most of all, being around both of you and your family has changed my life!

The people that work with you in your ministry are the most wonderful, genuine and warmest people I have ever met in my life. Thank you for helping me grow spiritually!

D.L.

Now what if this woman had read my books and listened to my tapes, but when she spent time in my presence was disappointed in the way I behaved? What if my family or I had been short-tempered, rude or unkind to her? We would not have had a positive influence on her; she may have even viewed us as hypocritical, and it could have hurt the cause of Jesus Christ.

Everybody wants to be loved, and God makes Himself known through His love.[13] For this reason I believe that nothing is more important to the heart of God than for us to focus on expressing His love in order to draw people to Jesus.

People are hungry, and they are looking for something real. When people taste the fruit in us and see that it is good,[14] they will want to find the Source of this fruit — this tree of life.[15] They will be ready to accept Jesus as the Way to form a personal, eternal relationship with God* and to experience the abundant, exceptional life on earth Jesus came to provide.[16]

God has given us gifts to help people, and we can use the gifts He has made available to us to a certain extent without having developed the fruit. When I first started ministering, I hadn't developed much fruit or even thought about it, as I mentioned before. I had a very strong gift of communication in order to teach and was operating in what I was called to do but with practically no fruit.

People may see the gifts operating in us, but most of the time they look closer, inspecting our fruit to see whether it is good before opening themselves up to receive from us. When we **show** people that what we have is real, **then** they will listen to what we say and be receptive to what the Holy Spirit wants to give them through us.

You can show people that what, actually Who, you have is real by responding with the good fruit to little incidents that happen in your

---

*To learn how to meet Jesus and form a personal relationship with God, see the prayer in the back of this book.

daily living. If someone bumps into you at the grocery store, steps on your toe or even rolls a cart over your foot, be nice about it. Learn how to respond good-naturedly, especially if you're prone to reacting with irritation or anger. To turn the situation into a pleasant experience, you could even laugh with the person, who certainly didn't intend to bump, step on or roll over you! People can see Jesus in your patient, even joyful, response to something as small as that.

If someone cuts in too closely in front of you in traffic and almost runs you off the road, you can use self-control to pray for the person instead of reacting with anger. However, if someone **intentionally** tries to run you off the road, you will need to take some kind of action besides simply responding with the fruit of patience or kindness! At a time like that you need the mature fruit of peace to keep your mind clear in order to hear the Holy Spirit tell you what to do. And you may also need His intervention to protect you. But under normal circumstances if you make a point of responding with kindness every time you have an opportunity, you will keep the way open for people to see and seek the Source of the love they find in you.

The Bible says that we are letters of Christ read by all men. We are the credentials of the ministry in which we've grown.[17] When people see our good fruit, as individuals and in our ministry together with other Christians, they are impressed with our credentials. They read in us the nature of the Person we represent, Jesus.

We learn how to develop the fruit by reading and applying the specifics the Bible gives us and by seeking God and praying. But we have already begun developing the fruit as our priority by simply making little choices throughout the day that display the fruit through our actions.

We are to go out into the world and let the Holy Spirit flow through us to show people God's love — His patience, kindness, goodness and the other fruit — and help people with His gifts. By focusing on the importance God places on developing the fruit of His Spirit, we will find that a door for the release of our gifts will swing wide open.

Follow the more excellent way of love. Receive God's love and let it flow out of you in its many forms and power to others.

Oh, taste and see that the LORD is good; blessed is the man who trusts in Him![18] Those who **trust** the Lord and take refuge in Him are happy and fortunate, so blessed that they are to be envied.[19] And *those who seek the LORD shall not lack any good thing.*[20]

Happy, fortunate, blessed, not lacking any good thing — these terms describe the exceptional type of life that God wants us to lead.

PART 1

KNOWN BY OUR FRUIT

CHAPTER 1

THE GOOD FRUIT WILL KEEP YOU WHERE THE GIFTS TAKE YOU

Many people whose gifts move them into a place they desire haven't developed the qualities they need to remain there. Or they may stay for a while at a certain level where their gifts took them but never move beyond it.

Through developing the character qualities of the fruit of the Spirit, already in those of us who are Christians, we are able to move into the blessed, exceptional type of life we truly desire. When we as Christians know what God has available for us and are open to receiving from Him, His Spirit will give us the power we need to develop the fruit and live the type of life God wants for us.[1]

I am grateful that God did not allow my gifts to expand until I let Him work with me for a few years on developing the fruit. When God dropped the teaching gift into me, it was strong. I taught then in just about the same way as I do now — years later. My gift moved me into a place of ministry as I had desired, but my ministry wasn't expanding in the way I wanted because I hadn't developed the fruit.

God gives us various gifts[2] to use, but He gives us the fruit of the Spirit to develop. When the Holy Spirit lives inside us, we have everything He has. His fruit is in us. The seed has been planted. In order to use the gifts in the most powerful way that God desires, we must allow the seed of the fruit to grow up and mature in us by cultivating it.

We can cultivate all the fruit by focusing on love, the first in the list of the nine fruit, and self-control, the last in the list. Love and self-control are like bookends that hold the rest in place. All of the fruit issue from love and actually are a form of love, but they are kept in place by self-control.

If you are concentrating on developing the fruit of love, as you walk through your day you won't become impatient with people. You won't be anything but kind. You will be good to people, supportive and faithful instead of being haughty or trying to appear better than others.

> ALL OF THE FRUIT ISSUE FROM LOVE AND ARE KEPT IN PLACE BY SELF-CONTROL.

If you aren't motivated by love, you will find that operating in the fruit is very difficult. But even when you are motivated to express God's love as a lifestyle, there will be times (**many** times when you first begin developing the fruit) when you won't feel like being patient, kind, joyful, peaceful or even nice at all! Those are the times that you need self-control in order to continue to respond with the fruit even though you don't feel like it.

If you need to develop this fruit of self-control, begin with simply making little choices throughout the day to respond with the fruit to situations you encounter, as discussed before. Pretty soon you will have formed a habit. At that stage, the seed of self-control in you will have grown into a little plant.

Once you have formed the habit, you won't be caught off guard as easily as when you first started developing self-control. When you are in that first stage of development, you can be walking along in the grocery store thinking everything is great. You can be in a good mood, thinking about how you don't have any problems right then and everything is wonderful. Then all of a sudden something minor will happen. Somebody will bump into you, step on your toe, roll a cart over your foot or make some other human mistake. And since you don't have mature fruit yet, you will respond in anger or impatience instead of choosing to respond good-naturedly with patience and perhaps even joy by laughing with the person over the incident. But don't despair, the more you practice displaying the fruit, the more mature they will become. At first you have to really try to control yourself, but eventually it will be very natural to respond the way Jesus would in a similar situation.

You may think, **Where did that come from? I thought I was nice and sweet.** Sometimes we think that we already have the fruit of the Spirit fully developed in us simply because we are Christians. But when we are caught off guard, or our fruit is "squeezed," we find out just how undeveloped the fruit in us is. These incidences are tests that are actually very good for us because they help us know the areas where we are weak and still need to grow.

SEED-SIZED FRUIT EQUALS SMALL-SIZED MINISTRY

When I began ministering in my gift, the fruit in me was definitely still in the seed-stage! And I operated that way for many years.

For five years I taught a weekly Bible study in my living room to a small group of thirty people. When I taught, I wore short shorts, just as short as I could get them. And I smoked — one cigarette after the other. I sat there on my living room floor blowing smoke in everybody's face the whole night while I was teaching the Bible!

I had no concern for the guests' feelings at all. It did not even occur to me that my smoking might make someone else uncomfortable or cause them to judge me adversely. There are many habits that can be detrimental to our Christian witness and I don't suppose that smoking is any worse than many others, but we should choose not to do things that are harmful to our health and the health of others. Wearing short shorts in that type of atmosphere was not a wise choice either but at that time in my life I simply did what I felt like doing without even considering how it might affect others. Love would have made different choices. It would have wisely chosen to do things that could not offend anyone.

You might be wondering how or why God would use me to teach His Word when my behavior was so immature, and I can certainly understand why you would. The only answer I can give is that God not only sees where we are right now, but He also sees where we came from and where we are going to end up. He knew my heart toward Him was right even though my behavior was very unwise. He gave me a space of time to change, and I am grateful for it.

People came to the Bible study because God's anointing was present, not because I was perfected yet. Most of them had the same problems I did, and we were trying to learn together. After a few months went by, I began to recognize that the Holy Spirit was dealing with me to dress differently and to stop smoking, as well as to make many other changes in my lifestyle habits. It was not easy to make the changes, but my love for Jesus helped me to press through the hard times of discipline.

Some people reading this book might say, "Well, hey, then why do I have to change if God used you like that when you had all those problems?"

If I hadn't allowed God to change me by working with Him to develop the fruit of self-control in many areas, I would still be sitting on my living room floor ministering to twenty-five or thirty people — or to only one or two who were sticking with me out of loyalty. If I hadn't allowed God to change me in preparation to fulfill His plan for me, I wouldn't have moved into my present position of ministering. I speak to large groups of people in different teaching conferences on a regular basis, and I am also able to reach people with God's love and His Word through a number of different Life In The Word outreaches all over the world. We are blessed to hear testimonies from people who tell us how God used this ministry to bring healing to them or transform their lives in other ways.

Yes, God will let us do some ministry before we allow Him to begin developing that seed of the fruit of the Spirit in us, but He won't loose us on the world until we mature a little. We won't accurately represent Him until we begin maturing and reflecting His character more and more! And as we develop the fruit, we learn how to draw more on Him to handle the growing responsibilities He gives us on our way to leading a more exceptional life.

CHAPTER 2

MOTIVATED BY OUR GIFTS

Many of the examples I am using from my life are related to public ministry because that is what God has called me to do. But in every area some very capable people who believe that they are called to do certain things become frustrated because they feel they don't have an open door to using their abilities. When they step out in an area, nothing works right.

There are many reasons why things don't always work out the way we desire. For one, God's timing is not our timing because He knows more about the situations than we do. But **sometimes**, as it was in my case, the reason is simply that the person hasn't developed any fruit.

Some people are taught certain good character traits as part of their upbringing; these are natural traits and not the same quality as the fruit of the Spirit of which I am speaking. To be honest, some people even though not believers in Jesus Christ may be naturally nice or easy to get along with; however, this is rare and always has its limits. God knows no limits; through His power and ability we can even learn to be kind to our enemies, which is one example of exceptional living — it is beyond normal; it is rare.

As a child I was not taught many good character traits; the examples I had were a bad influence rather than a good one. The Holy Spirit began to teach me when I accepted Jesus as my Savior and has never ceased since that time. I still have much to learn, but I have also made a lot of progress.

<u>MOTIVATED TO PRESS TOWARD THE FINISH LINE</u>

I really used to wonder why God gives gifts to immature people. One day I asked Him, "Why on earth do You do that?" As soon as I asked, God dropped the answer into my heart. If He had not put that gift and calling in me, I would never have been motivated to press toward the finish line. Most of us have such an intense desire to use our gifts that our gifts themselves motivate us to do whatever God tells us to do in order to be able to use them. Because God had filled me with certain gifts, I would do anything I understood God wanted me to do in order to use those gifts and fulfill that call. And that included developing the fruit of the Spirit!

If, as an immature Christian, I hadn't already had the gift of communication in me to begin preaching and teaching the Bible, I wouldn't have known what I was supposed to do — what my part was to be in the body of Christ.[1] And because God puts gifts in immature people, those people make many mistakes and messes while they grow in the knowledge of Him and develop His fruit, just like babies who start out in diapers make lots of messes on their way to maturity.

THE DIFFERENT GIFTS WORK TOGETHER

FOR THE COMMON GOOD

The Holy Spirit works different gifts in different people together to accomplish certain purposes.[2]

God gives certain gifts, different roles to fill, to people to help others grow. These ministry gifts are varied to help the body of believers grow up and work together in accomplishing God's work.[3] Of these roles some are *apostles (special messengers)*; others are *prophets (inspired preachers and expounders)*; others are *evangelists (preachers of the Gospel, traveling missionaries)*; others *pastors (shepherds of His flock)*; some are *teachers.*[4] The Bible also mentions administration gifts, helps, giving, exhortation, music and many others.

> THE HOLY SPIRIT WORKS DIFFERENT GIFTS IN DIFFERENT PEOPLE TOGETHER TO ACCOMPLISH CERTAIN PURPOSES.

Whether the gifts are the roles we fill to help other Christians grow[5] or the special endowments of supernatural energy operating through us listed in 1 Corinthians chapter 12,[6] they are given to us for the Holy Spirit to work them together in ministering *for the profit of all.*[7]

RECEIVE THE BLESSING OF ANOTHER PERSON'S GIFT

God has also given us different natural gifts to help us in ministering. And we will find that exercising them is fulfilling. If we spend our time wanting a gift we don't have, especially if we try to exercise one we don't have, we will find this to be a frustrating experience. And many people spend their entire lives doing just this!

I used to wish with all my heart that I could sing. In fact, it kind of aggravated me that I couldn't! I saw other preachers who could preach and sing — some could play instruments as well. I thought it would be the greatest thing to be able to preach for a little while, go out into the congregation and sing a song from the Lord to someone, then go back to the platform and preach a little more, and after a while, stop and lead a few praise songs to the Lord.

Once when I was thinking about that, the Lord impressed upon me, "You'd really like that if you could do it all. Then you wouldn't need anybody. And that's exactly why I didn't give it all to you!"

We need to do what God has given *us* to do, and let Him use other people to do what He wants *them* to do![8]

I used to make myself miserable wanting a gift like one a friend of mine had, while God had placed that gift in her for the benefit of others, including me! This friend, who used to travel with us, has a beautiful singing voice. It is one of those high soprano voices that sounds like it reverberates way out into the stratosphere somewhere when she hits those high notes. I used to really enjoy listening to her sing. One day when I was thinking, **Oh, God, I would love to be able to sing like that** . . . ! the Lord told me, "As long as you want what she's got, then you cannot enjoy what I have put in her for you as a gift."

We keep ourselves from fully enjoying the blessing of the gift God put in another person for our benefit — to build us up — by focusing on wanting a gift like it for ourselves! And not only that, by wanting something we don't have, we can become discontent. A disgruntled person who goes around with a bad attitude all the time doesn't bear good fruit.

If we are dissatisfied with the gifts God gave us, we won't give ourselves over completely to growing in them. We will miss the satisfaction God intends for us to find in ministering with others as the Holy Spirit works our varied gifts together for the common good, the purpose that God intends.

WORKS OF THE FLESH STUMP OUR GROWTH!

Envy and jealousy are works of the flesh rather than fruit of the Spirit.[9] The works of the flesh keep us from walking in step with the Spirit and growing and displaying His fruit.[10] Instead of coveting my friend's gift, I could have enjoyed it. I could have expressed my appreciation to God for blessing me with that gift in her. Then, refreshed by my friend's gift as God intended, I could have returned to fully concentrating on developing the gifts God gave me.

YOUR GIFT IS FOR A PURPOSE

John the Baptist came to tell people to prepare the way for the Lord.[11] That was his purpose on earth, and he knew it. But John's disciples were trying to incite him to jealousy over Jesus' ministry! They said, . . . *here He is baptizing too, and everybody is flocking to Him!*[12]

John responded to them by basically saying, "If He is doing that, then God has anointed Him to do it, and it's His time to do it. And if my time's up, then my time's up"! (John did not have a jealousy problem!) . . . *A man must be content to receive the gift which is given him from heaven; there is no other source.*[13]

Heaven is the only source for gifts. If God doesn't give you another gift, you won't get one. So if your gift is giving,[14] then give, and do it with singleness of mind, liberality and zeal. If your gift is helping,[15] then help somebody! You might as well be content and enjoy the gift you have. After you decide to be content and give yourself over to your gift completely, you will find that you do enjoy using it. And that enjoyment will grow as you continue to use and develop that gift. It is very important to find out what your gift is and use it — give yourself over to it.[16]

The goal of people who are mature in the fruit is to fit into place with the other members of the body or team to work together for the common good. Mature Christians know that faithfulness brings blessings[17] and that God is the One Who promotes.[18] People who mature in the fruit are good team members, easy to work with and valuable employees. People with these qualities find that their supervisors often want to promote them. There are many good reasons for developing the fruit of the Spirit!

CHAPTER 3

MOTIVATED (A LITTLE TOO MUCH) BY THE GIFTS

M any new Christians with immature fruit and a pure heart full of God's love apply their zeal to learning how to develop their fruit and serve the Lord well. Immature Christians start out spiritually like babies do physically on their way to growing up. They need their diapers changed, and when they fall down while learning to walk, they need help standing back up. They make a normal number of messes and mistakes, take a normal number of unsure steps as they grow; then after a while, they are out of diapers and are steady on their feet. They still need help along the way, including guidance from the Holy Spirit and believers He may choose to work through as they continue to grow, but they develop the fruit until they reach maturity.

Some immature Christians make quite a few more messes and mistakes and take a few more falls than they need to experience! Some of them spend years in the diaper- and learning-to-walk stage! But others, in their zeal and early attempts to use the gifts, don't always understand the purpose of their gifts. They may operate out of the wrong motivation — to look better or feel more important than other people.

The apostle Paul was addressing a similar situation when he said not to be ignorant concerning spiritual gifts.[1] One thing he apparently meant was, "Don't be ignorant of their purpose." People were operating in the gifts — zealously.[2] But Paul must have seen that some people were unaware of why. Some may have been trying to prophesy louder than other people to appear more spiritual, for example. Paul instructed them to redirect that zeal toward excelling in a way that would build up the church.[3] He was saying, "Hey, you're missing the point! God gave us the gifts for the good and profit of all, not for us to use to make ourselves look more spiritual!"

One of the ways Christians mature and are guided along the way is through the people filling the roles of the ministry gifts in their body of believers, as we saw.[4] I have discovered that Christians who have not worked on the process of developing the fruit before entering another group — a church, a ministry or other organization — are trouble and dangerous.

Because of their gifts, immature Christians sometimes become filled with pride[5] and want to be used only in certain ways. Instead of coming in with an attitude of serving, they often describe all their wonderful gifts, the number of things they want to do and the roles that they ought to fill. That type of behavior really turns off leaders fast. Leaders know that they would have plenty of messes to clean up made by those people who haven't developed enough fruit to handle themselves properly in those roles.

Rather than fitting in and contributing their part to accomplish the work God has for that portion of the body (or the common goal in any setting), immature Christians want to draw attention to themselves. They are usually difficult to work with and can disrupt the effectiveness of a ministry by disturbing other people and the workflow.

Those immature Christians are acting on the first part of the Scripture that tells us to *earnestly desire and zealously cultivate the greatest and best gifts,* but without the motivation of love Paul referred to in his statement in the second part of the verse: *And yet I will show you a still more excellent way.*[6] When people want to use the gifts for their own reasons instead of out of a desire to show God's love and help people, they cause problems and create strife.

No matter how great people's gifts are, they won't be able to be in, or stay in, a position to use those gifts without having developed the fruit.

INSTEAD OF BLOWING YOUR HORN, DEVELOP THE FRUIT

If I hire somebody who in a week or two starts telling me how wonderful they are, I might let them sit there and stew for a while until they deal with that pride problem. In my ministry, they won't be promoted too much until we check their fruit. They need a little breaking in. This doesn't mean that they don't have gifts. But the point that I want to make in this book is that our gifts aren't worth two cents if we haven't developed the fruit.

Sometimes people come up to me in a conference and tell me that God sent them to minister to me. They tell me that they are to become involved in my ministry and that they know God will use them to be an enormous blessing to me. I tell every single one of them: "OK, then start coming to my meetings and sit in them for a while to soak up the Word."

After I say that, I usually learn right away whether they actually did hear from God and have the maturity to do what they say they should be doing. Their answer is usually something like, "Oh, well, no, that isn't what God wants me to do. God wants me to work on your team and be close to you. I'm supposed to do things personally for you and be with you." Because they think that they heard a word from the Lord that I am supposed to do what they tell me, they are offended when I won't immediately do what they say. And they think that I'm the one not hearing from God instead of them.

> OUR GIFTS AREN'T WORTH TWO CENTS IF WE HAVEN'T DEVELOPED THE FRUIT.

Mature Christians with the right intent aren't offended by my response. They know why I need to take that stand. I wouldn't bring them into my life, start eating all my meals with them and give them a high position on my staff without knowing them, checking their fruit or receiving confirmation from God that what they told me is true. They would agree with my response and let God promote them instead of trying to promote themselves.

I would have no common sense whatsoever and would not be using godly wisdom to let everybody who tells me that they should become involved closely with me, move right into my personal life without watching them for a while and checking their fruit. If I'm looking for someone to fill that kind of key position in my ministry, especially if I will be around the person quite a bit, I ask all kinds of questions, look over their resume, history and recommendations. Then I usually place them somewhere else in the organization for a while to test them by seeing how they handle themselves.

I find out if they're walking in love. I make sure that they have peace and joy. I look for stability — whether they are in control of their emotions. I watch to see how they handle themselves when they have personal trials or when I correct them or say no to something they want. I watch how they handle strife when it comes in the ministry. Do they join in as part of it or do they stand against and resist it?

When I find someone who passes all those tests, it's like finding a bar of gold. There are many people these days who appear to be mature Christians who are not. But there are also many wonderful, mature Christians who are dedicated to serving God's purposes. To recognize them we need to know that it is necessary to judge people's fruit and how to do it.

Some people think they need to blow their own horn. They don't — they just need to develop their fruit. The tree is known, recognized and judged by its fruit.

An orange tree wouldn't need to stand there and announce over and over, "I'm an orange tree; I'm an orange tree; look at me — I'm an orange tree . . ."! If you see an orange tree, you know the type of tree it is by its fruit. If the tree is producing oranges, it's an orange tree!

THE GREATER GIFTS

The immature Christian also doesn't understand the reason that some gifts are greater than others. When we consider that God's love is the basis for moving in the gifts and that the Holy Spirit works the gifts together for the common good, for the profit of all, we can begin to see why some of the spiritual gifts are described as being greater. In another Scripture in which Paul again urges to first pursue love in desiring the spiritual gifts, he begins to discuss a greater gift. *Pursue love, yet desire earnestly spiritual gifts, but especially that you may prophesy.*[7]

Paul is discussing a particular setting for the operation of this gift — when the church is assembled. Because everything should be done for edification[8] — done in a way that builds up the church —

a greater gift in a group setting would be one that edifies the greatest number of people. Of the gifts, prophesying would bring the greatest benefit — for the common good, the profit of all — to the largest number of people in an assembly. In this context Paul says that someone who prophesies is greater than someone who speaks in tongues, unless they interpret the tongues, . . . *so that the church may receive edifying.*[9]

If an immature Christian motivated by the desire to look spiritual is speaking in tongues in a group setting without anyone interpreting, people unfamiliar with the gifts — uninformed or unbelievers — won't know what is happening. They certainly won't be edified or built up. Not only will they not understand what the believer is saying — they will probably say that the person is out of their mind![10] People are not impressed with this kind of behavior; they are impressed when a Christian offers them something from God out of a heart of love.

Even though Paul wished that they all spoke in tongues[11] and said that he spoke in tongues more than all of them,[12] his motivation was to teach them which gift should be desired in this situation — one that would be of the greatest benefit for the common good. When the church is assembled, prophesying will profit more people than speaking in tongues, unless interpreted,[13] because, *One who speaks in a tongue edifies himself; but one who prophesies edifies the church.*[14] No one but the person speaking in tongues will be edified unless the tongue is interpreted because no one will understand what is being said. The person is speaking to God rather than man.[15]

If the tongue is interpreted, then the church will be edified. But when someone prophesies in a group meeting, everyone can be edified because everyone understands what the person is saying. Even people who don't understand what spiritual gifts are will be able to receive ministry from this gift. And 1 Corinthians 14:3 tells us that prophesying always speaks to men for *edification, and exhortation, and comfort.*[16] Prophesying is for building up and for constructive spiritual progress, strengthening, encouragement and consolation.[17]

God's motivation in giving the gifts is love. Out of love He makes the gifts available to help people. This is the *more excellent way.* As we have seen, earnestly desiring the best gifts for the sake of seeming more spiritual than other people is not the most excellent way.

When we as mature Christians are motivated by God's love to help people, we are motivated to use the gifts to fulfill God's purpose. Out of compassion to be able to help people in a powerful way, we want the Holy Spirit to minister the gifts through us for the

> OUT OF LOVE GOD MAKES THE GIFTS AVAILABLE TO HELP PEOPLE.
>
>

betterment, progress and enjoyment of others. And we earnestly desire for the particular gift to operate through us which will best meet someone's need at the moment.

CHAPTER 4

BEARING GOOD FRUIT FROM THE INSIDE OUT

Being the same kind of Christian on the inside as we give the appearance of being on the outside is a serious matter. Many people are searching for God today, and there are many teachings about how to find Him that sound right. People may adopt one of these without realizing that they have not found the One True God. When people are attracted to our fruit, we need to make sure that it tastes as good as it looks. Then when people pluck it, they will see Jesus in us. We will be able to introduce Him, their only hope of salvation, as the real and only way to God.

FRUIT THAT LOOKS GOOD BUT IS BAD

In today's society with so much importance placed on the way things look, there are many people who have fruit that appears to be good but in fact it is bad. One time when I saw some big, beautiful oranges in the grocery store, I decided to buy one. From the price, I just knew that orange would taste as good as it looked and be filling. It looked like a meal in itself, and I was hungry. I thought, **That is the most gorgeous orange I've ever seen, and I'm paying the dollar for it!**

When I went outside to my car, I peeled that beautiful thing and bit into it. It was as dry and tasteless as it could be. The inside was the direct opposite of what I had expected. I thought, **And I paid a dollar for this?**

I refuse to be a dry-on-the-inside but polished, beautiful-on-the-outside Christian who draws people with good-looking fruit, but has only dried-up, old, tasteless nothing to give them when they try to pluck it. I know about this because I used to be like that tasteless orange.

FRUIT THAT LOOKS GOOD BUT IS IMMATURE

I had been a Christian a long time when God impressed upon me that I should concentrate my energy on developing the fruit of the Spirit. Before that, I didn't have a clue about the importance of a Christian's inner life. I thought that the important thing was for my family to appear to be proper Christians. I was all caught up in that. My husband, Dave, was an elder in the church. I was on the church board. Our kids went to Christian schools. Our social life revolved around church. We had Christian bumper stickers on our cars. I wore a Jesus pin, carried my Bible around and listened to teaching tapes — all the outward identifying signs. We walked into church looking like the model joy-filled, peaceful family. But before we walked into the church, we had spent the morning in a state of complete turmoil!

Everything bad that could happen usually happened on Sunday morning before church. Somebody would lose something. One of the kids would spill something at breakfast or get mad about something and start throwing a tantrum. I would yell at Dave and blame him for making us late because I thought he should be helping me more. Then Dave and I would start arguing and fight all the way to church. But once we arrived in the parking lot and started walking toward the front door, we pulled out our happy, peaceful-looking church faces, slapped them on and walked in saying to people, "Praise the Lord! Hallelujah! How are you? We're just fine." During one service, I remember standing next to Dave and while I was sweetly singing the praise songs to the Lord with him, I was thinking, **If Dave thinks I'm cooking him anything to eat today, he's got another thing coming!**

I realized years later that when all this turmoil happens, it is Satan trying to upset the entire household to keep us out of peace. He tries to upset us before we go to a service to keep us from hearing and receiving from God. And many people identify with this type of experience! But at the time I made everything as difficult as possible by behaving out of a state of complete spiritual immaturity and throwing bad fruit around in the midst of it.

God sees our heart[1] and is not impressed by an act we put on while our heart is far from Him. In Isaiah 29:13 the Lord speaks of people whose worship is useless because they worship Him with their lips while their heart is far from Him. I finally had to look at my heart attitude, not just my outward acts. God eventually requires that of each one of us. We must become honest with ourselves and with God or we will not continue to grow as believers.

FRUIT THAT LOOKS GOOD THAT IS GOOD

The thing that caused me to be willing to allow God to change me into being more like Jesus was seeing that the good fruit my husband displayed was real. I received good teaching about God in church, which helped me and gave me a good foundation. Instruction is very important. Assembling with other believers in church is very important.[2] But the thing that really made a difference in my life was not so much the teaching or Dave taking me to church every Sunday, but the fruit I saw in Dave's life behind closed doors when we weren't on public display as the proper Christian family. I wanted to have in my life what he had in his.

When I became angry at him, he was still kind to me. When I made a big display about how upset I was in front of him, he wouldn't let me upset him. He had made a decision to love me. If I wanted to receive it, the love was there. If I wanted to pout all day and be miserable, he was staying in peace and keeping his joy. He said that he couldn't do anything about my decision to be unhappy, but he wasn't going to be unhappy with me. He told me, "If you want to stay mad all day, then stay mad all day. But I'm going to enjoy my family; I'm going to enjoy my kids. I'm going to watch the football game and have a good time. I'm going to go out and eat. I'm going to enjoy my life, and when you want to enjoy your life with us, we're here."

After he said something like that, I really became infuriated because unhappy people want to make everyone else unhappy! But one of the best things he did for me was to remain stable. If he had let me make him miserable, there is a good possibility that Dave and I would both still be sitting around somewhere being miserable and not accomplishing much for God. But because Dave kept showing me joy and peace, I was finally so hungry for what he had that I became willing to let God change my life. We need to **be** something in front of people that they see and want.

EVERYTHING BEARS FRUIT

Everything was created to bear fruit. If you use a Bible concordance and begin to study the words *fruit, fruitful* and *unfruitful*, you will be amazed at the number of references there are in the Bible to the giving forth of fruit. For example, in the very beginning of the Bible, God said to Adam and Eve, *Be fruitful, multiply, and fill the earth.*[3]

What exactly does the Bible mean when it speaks of fruitful? One definition of it is *fertile.*[4] Of course, the word *fertile* has several meanings. If a woman is fertile, that means that she has the ability to conceive and give birth to a child. If a piece of land is fertile, that means it has the power to bring forth something that can be harvested to meet the needs of human beings. If your life is bringing forth anything that can be harvested to meet the needs of others when they pluck that fruit, then your life is fruitful, just as God intended it to be.

You and I are the fruitbearers of the kingdom of God. When you attend a conference and soak up God's Word being taught, you have a right to expect some good fruit to grow in your life as a result because you sowed your time. When you work all week, you expect the fruit of a paycheck. Every day, our day should bear some kind of good fruit.

Some people feel as though they have been plucked to the point of having no fruit left on their tree. They say something like: "Everybody I'm around wants something out of me. I'm tired of being the only person who is nice. I'm tired of always being the one to apologize or of always being the one to give in. I don't know if I have enough fruit left for all the people around me who are picking on me."

> EVERY DAY, OUR DAY SHOULD BEAR SOME KIND OF GOOD FRUIT.

The next time you want someone to stop picking on you, realize that God is expecting you to have some fruit for people to pick. For a long time I didn't understand the story of Jesus cursing the fig tree because it didn't have any fruit. Actually, I felt sorry for the fig tree!

NO FRUIT COMES FROM A PHONY TREE

The fig tree was standing there being a fig tree, as it was supposed to be doing. Because Jesus was hungry and the fig tree didn't have any figs, . . . *He said to it, Never again shall fruit grow on you! And the fig tree withered up at once.*[5]

One day when I was reading this story in *The Amplified Bible*, I finally understood the point. When Jesus was coming back to the city in the early dawn, . . . *He was hungry. And as He saw one single leafy fig tree above the roadside, He went to it but He found nothing but leaves on it [seeing that in the fig tree the fruit appears at the same time as the leaves]. . . .*[6]

With most fruit trees, if there are leaves, there is fruit under the leaves. Jesus saw the leaves on the fig tree and went to it for something to eat because He was hungry. When He saw that it had leaves but no fruit, He cursed it because it was a phony. Where there are leaves, there is supposed to be fruit!

If our lives revolve around the church and we have Christian bumper stickers on our cars, wear Jesus pins, carry our Bibles around, sit by ourselves at lunch at work to read our Bibles, have plaques hanging on our walls with Scriptures about the fruit of the Spirit on them and listen to teaching tapes and say, "Praise the Lord! Hallelujah!" but don't ever have time to help anybody else or even show kindness, we're like the fig tree with leaves but no fruit.

If someone asks us to do something and we answer, "Can't you see I'm trying to read my Bible?" or "Get out of here and leave me alone — I'm praying!" or "Don't talk to me — I'm having a visitation from God!" we have leaves but no fruit.

If a friend calls and says, "Could you do me a favor and watch my kids for half an hour? I've had a problem and need to run somewhere quickly," and we respond, "I'd like to help you, but I just can't right now. I've got plans — I'm sorry. I hope you understand." If we could have changed our plans but were simply too selfish to do so, we're like that phony fig tree.

People with a spiritual outward appearance but no fruit are hard to get along with and never allow themselves to be inconvenienced by anybody else. I know because I used to be that way. But I decided a long time ago that I am not going to be a phony Christian.

I want people to say, "Joyce and Dave are genuine. Their ministry is real. Every time I see them, they are doing behind the scenes what they preach. They weren't one way with me and another way with somebody else."

It's so important that we bear good fruit. It's especially important that if we appear to have good fruit, we actually have it. Jesus called the Pharisees a *brood of vipers* because they spoke good things when they were evil.[7] They were phony like the fig tree.

If we have the outward appearance of being Christians, the many people searching for God will be watching us. They will want to know Jesus like we do when they see that our fruit is as good inside as it looks on the outside. We will be the ambassadors for Christ that He intends us to be.[8]

CHAPTER 5

INSPECTING FRUIT AND DISCERNING DECEPTION

God intends for us to lead the type of exceptional life in which everything we do prospers. We can live this way when we have mature fruit. Instead of being like the phony fig tree that Jesus cursed because it had no fruit, the Bible tells us we can be like a tree firmly planted by the rivers of water that brings forth fruit in season, and whatever we do will prosper.[1]

Developing the fruit is important and is a priority, so that we will be like that tree by the water, ready to give good fruit when plucked. Because there is a great deal of deception these days, it is also important for us to know how to judge other people's fruit and discern other people's intentions. We need to know how to determine with whom we should form relationships — whether in ministry, in business or in society.

INSPECTING THE FRUIT

Before becoming involved with or contributing to the ministry of someone I don't know well, I ask God to show me the person's heart, and I judge the person's fruit. For example, I had heard many good things about a certain minister but didn't know him very well, even though a number of years ago he attended the same church Dave and I did. I knew that thousands and thousands of people had received the Lord all over the world as a result of his music ministry teams and other outreaches of his ministry.

He lives in Tulsa, Oklahoma, and had been asked to minister at a pastors' conference in a church there. When he arrived, he found out that only twenty pastors were attending. One of the twenty was the man who buys our media time.

The minister told his story about what was going on in China. Our media man was so moved that he was in tears by the time he finished speaking and said to him, "Dave and Joyce Meyer need to hear this story. Will you go to St. Louis and tell them what you just told us?"

He didn't know us very well either but came to St. Louis anyway. As we were talking, I said to the Lord, "Help me see this man's heart and what You've called him to do."

As I listened to him talk, I thought, **It is so awesome that he has such character — such heart and integrity — that he went to the pastors' conference to talk to twenty people.** He has spoken widely on praise and worship. Between the late-sixties and the mid-eighties, his music ministry teams traveled around the world, with a large ministry to then-communist countries, sometimes ministering to audiences of nearly 250,000 people! Yet, he went and talked to twenty pastors.

This minister did have a need. In order to release several million Bibles in China, he needed several thousand dollars for something that needed to be completed first. Another ministry was joining him to pay another part of it, but they had only a certain amount of time before they needed the entire amount. They were getting close to the wire. We have a percentage of money that we set aside for world outreach and, praise God, we were able to meet the need of his ministry. We were able to be a part in helping to release several million Bibles in China.

Some ministers with a similar-sized ministry to his, but without similar character qualities, wouldn't have spoken to that small group of people. Or, after arriving to discover only twenty people were attending, would have given an excuse and said, "Maybe someone else could cover this."

When we have the character to do what we say we are going to do, to treat people right and keep a right attitude about things, God will always come through. Whether it's a back door, side door, window, roof or some other way, He will bless us and meet our needs.

LOOK AT THE HEART

To judge a person's fruit, we need to know specifically what to examine. Otherwise, because we are so used to forming conclusions based on the way things appear, we may examine the wrong fruit. For instance, we may incorrectly decide that a person's fruit is good from looking at what they have or haven't done, the type of things they own or even the size of their ministry.

A few years ago one of the questions I often heard ministers ask other ministers when meeting for the first time was, "Do you travel out of the country?" If the answer was no, the response was, "You haven't?" as if you weren't a real minister with an effective ministry for God if you hadn't traveled to three or four foreign places! Your fruit was judged as good or bad based on whether you had traveled out of the country.

I knew at that time that I was called to be right here teaching the people in the United States. That didn't mean I didn't care about the people in other countries, but God had not called me to minister overseas in the beginning of my ministry. Now, I understand why — the outreaches of my ministry today are touching the world in a totally different way than I would have imagined. Even though I do travel overseas now, I am also ministering to the world through those outreaches themselves, including a lot of foreign TV. God was leading me at that time to remain in the United States most of the time because I was developing a foundation for our ministry that would be large enough to eventually reach the world. Had I been moved by what people expected of me instead of what the Lord was leading me to do, I would not be able to minister all around the world today by television and other outreaches. As an example of what I am saying, just yesterday our oldest son, David, and another minister left for India and Africa to host major youth conferences that our ministry will completely fund.

Often we are provoked by others to try to bear fruit in some area before it is ripe. As we all know, unripe fruit is just about as useless as no fruit at all. Remember that there is a season for everything, and everything is beautiful in its time according to Ecclesiastes chapter 3, but the opposite would be true if it is out of the right time.

Instead of looking only at what people do, we need to inspect their fruit by looking at the attitude and type of character people display while they are doing what they do. The minister from Tulsa I mentioned previously has a very effective overseas ministry. But instead of judging his fruit on the basis of his travel and ministry to foreign countries, we see the evidence of his good fruit first in his character qualities and attitude toward serving God. As we saw before, a person's motivation, the person's earnest desires, shows us a great deal. We have a good indication that a person's fruit is mature, good from the inside out and real, when we see the person operating out of a desire to express God's love by looking for ways to combine their gifts with other people's to help accomplish God's particular purpose.

DISCERNING THE INTENT

> A PERSON'S MOTIVATION SHOWS US A GREAT DEAL ABOUT THE PERSON'S FRUIT.

We must remember that it is important not to be so awed by a person's gift that we forget to judge their fruit. If we forget to look at the character and motivation of a person behind the gift, we may be led astray. I must repeat: Don't be so awed or impressed by a person's gifts, their charismatic personality or their abilities in any area that you become willfully blind to warning signs that something is wrong. I recently encountered a sad situation in which many people were devastated by the fall of a minister whom they greatly looked up to and perhaps in some instances even idolized, which of course is wrong. They all shared with me that they had known for a long time that the man often did not tell the truth, but somehow they ignored that warning sign because of other impressive things about him.

Not telling the truth is a character problem, and we must always look to the true character of an individual in judging the real fruit of their life.

Another big warning sign that a person has character problems is when they don't keep their word. I refuse to be in relationship with people who don't do what they say they will do. If we cannot trust people, how can we form real relationships with them?

In teaching people not to be ignorant of the spiritual gifts,[2] Paul was telling people to operate in the gifts for the right reason. But I believe he was also pointing out that the people were paying so much attention to other people's gifts that they weren't discerning the character of the person behind the gift.

Paul was talking to people who had worshipped mute idols before becoming Christians. He was teaching them how to recognize when someone is speaking by the true God so that they would not be led astray. He taught them that no one speaking under the power and influence of the Holy Spirit of God can ever say Jesus is accursed. And no one can really say that Jesus is their Lord except by the Holy Spirit.[3]

Paul was explaining that no matter how spiritual people appear to be — how impressive their gifts are, what they can do, who they know, how much money they have, what they say to you to compliment you to try to be close to you — to look beyond that. They may be dedicated to serving themselves instead of Jesus. They may not be of God at all — His Spirit may not live in them.

Jesus was warning His followers not to be deceived by the way people appear when He said to beware of false prophets who come dressed as sheep but inside are devouring wolves.[4] Jesus told them, *A good tree cannot bear bad fruit, nor can a bad tree bear good fruit.*[5]

Whether its fruit is good or bad, a tree is known by its fruit! You might be thinking about someone you know who seems to have many character deficits, yet their life or ministry still bears good fruit. That may be true to an extent, but it is really the Word of God that is bearing the fruit. God's Word does not return void no matter who speaks it. However, eventually this type of individual will cause real problems, and many people will be hurt. We can easily avoid much of the pain we encounter in life by being good fruit inspectors and choosing our friends and associates more wisely.

TAKE HEED NOT TO BE DECEIVED

Jesus said, *Take heed that no man deceive you.*[6] The Bible teaches us how not to be deceived. We should take full advantage of this knowledge God has given us because the Bible also tells us that in the last days deception will become so rampant that even God's select people could be deceived.[7] There will be people who say they are the Christ, the Messiah, and false prophets who will deceive and lead many people astray. They will even show great signs and wonders.[8] It will be pretty confusing to tell who is who

> WHETHER ITS FRUIT IS GOOD OR BAD, A TREE IS KNOWN BY ITS FRUIT!

and what is what. This shows how important it is to become fruit inspectors. God has told us in advance and given us the means to prepare to protect us.

To avoid deception, I don't follow anybody or become involved with their ministry — no matter how nice someone's sheep's clothing looks, no matter how polished and professional the person seems — until I've checked their fruit. Just as people come up to me in a conference to tell me that God wants them to be in a top-level position in my ministry, sometimes people come up who want to pray for me by laying hands on me in order to impart something to me spiritually. I tell them something like, "I don't want to hurt or offend you, but I'm not going to let you lay hands on me. You may be a wonderful person and Christian and your town's greatest intercessor, and if God told you to pray for me, please do! But don't you realize that because I don't know you, it would be unwise to allow you to lay hands on me. You see there is a transfer of power from one individual to another through prayer and the laying on of hands. You might remember that Jesus laid His hands on people and healed them or blessed them, and the apostles did the same."

I'm very nice when I respond because I don't want to hurt people, and I understand that immature Christians do make mistakes while they are trying to learn how to follow God and grow up. But I don't let anyone I don't know lay hands on me or anyone else in my meetings. My ushers are instructed to stop people who try to start laying hands on people and praying. I have a responsibility to the people who have come to protect them as much as possible from any harm.

DISCERNING GOOD (AND EVIL)

Sometimes we meet a person who seems to have good fruit, but we have a gut feeling that something about the person isn't right. It is very important to take heed and follow up to see if we are discerning correctly instead of ignoring the feeling. But it is also very important not to make decisions, especially radical ones, based on every little feeling. We may have a strange impression about someone because the person's personality reminds us of someone else with a similar personality whom we had problems with in the past. Or there may be something else that we don't like about the person that has nothing to do with discernment.

We need a great deal of discernment, and the Bible says we can have it if we seek it. God wants us to ask Him for wisdom, knowledge and understanding.[9] He wants to give us discretion and discernment.[10]

We can see how much God wants us to draw on His wisdom and discernment in the example of His response to Solomon's request after Solomon had become king. In a dream (which came to pass) Solomon asked God for the ability to *discern between good and evil* so that he would have *an understanding heart* to judge God's people. God was so pleased with Solomon's request that He gave him a wise and understanding heart unlike anyone else's in the past or to come. God also gave Solomon the riches and honor he hadn't requested — riches and honor greater than any other king's in Solomon's lifetime. And God also told Solomon that He would lengthen his days if he kept God's statutes and commandments.[11]

To develop the fruit of the Spirit is our priority. But it is also important to God for us to desire and pray for the *discerning* or *the distinguishing of spirits*,[12] one of the spiritual gifts, to operate in our lives. Discerning between good and evil means discerning whether a person's intent is good or evil, right or wrong, in most of the situations we encounter. Sometimes people become out of balance by overspiritualizing every feeling they have or "discerning" that something is wrong in every situation. Discernment isn't only for evil; it is for good as well. This means recognizing the good in people, not just looking for evil.

By making a decision that we will not be impressed only by the way things look, we can keep from being deceived. Instead of judging a person's fruit as good only because it appears to be, we can use self-control and patience to take the time to seek God for discernment; then, we can closely inspect the fruit.

LISTEN WITH YOUR SPIRIT

Things that we cannot understand with our mind, we can discern with our spirit.[13] God intends for us to use our minds for reasoning and common sense. But we can overdo reasoning by trying to figure out things to the point of becoming confused.[14] Something that I've learned about discernment is that we need to shut off our reasoning, get "out of our head" a little and listen to our spirit. This is especially important when the impressions or promptings from our spirit are telling us the opposite of the way a situation or person appears to be.

If you have an impression that something is not right about someone who appears to be mature and following God wholeheartedly, follow up on it by watching the person's behavior and listening to what they say to see their heart intent. "Watching and waiting" is the best advice I can give concerning making decisions about someone's true character.

WATCH THE BEHAVIOR

I mentioned the type of characteristics I watch for in judging the fruit of people I hire for key positions. And in judging anyone's fruit, even if the person has a big ministry with wonderful praise and worship music and produces a tremendous magazine, we should look at the type of fruit the person displays behind the scenes.

Now, we all become irritated occasionally or a little impatient, and we certainly don't respond perfectly with the love of God at all times. But we see indications of immature, bad or no fruit if a person has a bad temper or wants to have everything their way all the time. The person often becomes angry and impatient with people, wants to control everything or is happy only if they are the only one getting all the attention.

Just watch and wait. God will expose their fruit. Even if the person was well known, all of a sudden the phony or rotten tree behind the fruit will be exposed.

LISTEN FOR THE ATTITUDE

The Bible gives us a way to spot fairly quickly in some circumstances whether a person's fruit is immature, bad or nonexistent (as with a false Christ, a false prophet or someone else not from God). It shows us how to look at the person's heart intent by listening to what the person says. . . . *For out of the abundance of the heart the mouth speaks.*[15]

50

The verse above and the one below tell us that we can learn a lot about people just by listening to them.

A good man out of the good treasure of his heart brings forth good things, and an evil man out of the evil treasure brings forth evil things.
MATTHEW 12:35 NKJV

> WE CAN LEARN WHAT A PERSON HAS IN THEIR HEART BY LISTENING TO WHAT THEY SAY.

I've always been a big talker, but I've been learning in the last few years to listen to people more and talk less. By listening, you learn a great deal about the type of fruit a person has, which is especially helpful if you are meeting the person for the first time.

Someone who talks only about money and things has a problem with greed. If you form a relationship with someone who puts a negative edge on everything, you're in for trouble. Someone who talks excessively about things that are wrong with people, churches, organizations — their pastor, their boss, church leadership, church programs, the government — has a critical, judgmental spirit. If you let a person like that into your life by becoming a friend, that person will also begin saying negative things about you. No matter how good or perfect you try to be around someone like that, at some point they will start finding things wrong with you.

I've had those kinds of friends, and I don't want any more of them. I've had enough pressure in my life; I don't need any more from friends like they were! They wanted me to be perfect. No one is capable of being a perfect friend. If I'm your friend, once in a while I will disappoint you. If you sit under my ministry, I won't be a perfect minister or teacher either.

We need friends who will give us space in obeying God and in making mistakes along the way. We need friends who will do what the Bible says and let love cover a multitude of sins[16] as they walk in love with us.

When I've had an impression that something isn't right about someone, I follow up on it by watching them and listening to them. About 90 percent of the time, what I felt turns out to be right. But even when I'm not right, many times God will shed light on something and teach me something that helps me discern more accurately in the future.

CHAPTER 6

FRUIT FOR THE GOOD TIMES AND IN RESERVE FOR OTHER TIMES

E ven in the midst of the extreme events happening in our world
today, God wants us to lead the exceptional, abundant type of
life He intends for us. And in these times that many will find
confusing, He wants us to know how to let our lives be a witness to
others and how to minister to them.

Peace and joy and the other fruit are given to us to draw on, not
just in good times, but all the time. When we work on developing
the fruit in the good times, we have a reserve to draw on in difficult
and critical times. A mature Christian knows how to draw on the
peace that surpasses understanding[1] in any situation from the Prince
of Peace,[2] Jesus the Peacemaker, Who lives inside us. A believer
mature in the fruit of joy knows how to be steady and stable no
matter what the circumstances.

One reason I am writing this book is that God impressed upon
me how important it is for people to concentrate on developing the

fruit of the Spirit in order to prepare to handle themselves properly in times of crisis, should crises come. We find out how far we have to go in developing the fruit when we are caught off guard and our fruit is "squeezed," as when someone is rude or hurts us in some other way. Because most of us have our fruit "squeezed" about a dozen times a day, it is so important to develop the fruit of the Spirit!

I've been studying the love walk and the fruit of the Spirit for nearly fifteen years. I spend a great deal of time meditating on Scriptures about love and reading the many books I have on that subject. I like to teach about the fruit of the Spirit and any subjects related to it. And one reason that I spend so much time on the fruit is that I really need to study it. I couldn't walk in the fruit consistently if I didn't! I have to work at it.

Some people are naturally nice, and ministers are supposed to be especially nice and kind. I would like to be able to relate that when I wake up in the morning, I open my eyes and automatically smile, sit up and begin singing praises to the Lord and speaking blessings out over my husband. But with the type of strong personality I have, merely waking up in the morning can sometimes automatically squeeze my fruit!

My husband, on the other hand, is one of those people who wakes up happy. Every day for the thirty-five years we have been married, he gets up so happy he's whistling. As soon as he opens his eyes, everything seems great to him. I just know what he is thinking about any situation that might be a concern: **Problem? No, I just cast my care upon the Lord because I know that He cares for me and will work everything out for the good of those who love Him and are called to His purpose.**[3] Of course, what he is thinking is absolutely true, but I really have to work to turn my thoughts into that kind of attitude when I first wake up.

When I get up, Dave says, "Good morning. How are you?"

I've learned not to tell him, "OK," because he says, "OK? Aren't you good? Aren't you excellent? Aren't you wonderful?"

I tell him, "I'm good," knowing my feelings will catch up with me when I am fully awake.

Some of us who at times fight off a bad mood (especially if we wake up that way) know that if someone comes in who is completely happy and positive right then, we also have to fight off the urge to jump up and scream, "Leave me alone!"

One day I was having a really good day. When I woke up the next morning, I felt really good — I had had a good night's sleep; I felt good physically; I was excited about the way the meetings had gone during our recent conference; everything seemed great.

Dave said, "How are you this morning?"

I said, "Good."

He said, "Good! Wow! We're making progress!"

I may not be where I need to be, but thank God I am making progress!

Most of us need to spend time studying the fruit because the flesh is strong. Even after meditating on the Scripture passages on patience, listening to teaching tapes on patience for two weeks and exuding patience in every situation we encounter, we can still get in the car and yell, "You idiot! How did you ever get a driver's license? People like you shouldn't be allowed out on the highway!" when another driver cuts in front of us.

Sometimes I have felt like a spiritual Jekyll and Hyde. I can be in the midst of behaving great and suddenly change over some irritating incident.

DEVELOPING THE FRUIT IS WELL WORTH THE EFFORT

The majority of us have to work at developing and displaying the fruit consistently, and it is hard work. But I'm writing this book to tell you that it's worth it. To live the happy, fortunate type of life that is so blessed it is to be envied, in which you lack nothing and everything you set your hand to prospers — it is worth it. To live the type of life (that comes from developing the fruit) in which you know you are doing what you were created to do and experience the joy that comes from living this way — it is worth it. Yes, this type of life is so blessed it is to be envied, but no one needs to envy it because they can have a similar type of life too.

> THE HARD WORK OF DEVELOPING AND DISPLAYING THE FRUIT IS WORTH THE EFFORT.

The Amplified Bible says that the fruit of the Spirit is *the work which His presence within accomplishes.*[4] The fruit that is manifest in our life is what will change the world around us. Every once in a while we need to look at ourselves and say, "Everybody is going to know me by my fruit," and take a look at what kind of yield is coming from our life. We need to examine how stable we are in tense situations. Looking at ourself as a fruit tree, how much fruit can be picked before we find we have no more? I believe we can grow to the point of never running out of good fruit to display no matter what is going on in our lives.

If we are not producing a very big yield, God will come in and prune us. He cuts us back for greater growth. After I spent years praying for the gifts to operate in my ministry, God answered by dealing with me to develop the fruit, and He began pruning me. God had in mind for me a ministry through which I could help lots and lots of people, but He could not let my ministry grow until He knew that He could trust me in every kind of situation. He didn't want me out there hurting thousands of people. He also didn't want me to make a fool out of myself and give Him a bad reputation! So He waited and pruned me, waited some more and pruned me and waited some more. He kept pruning me until I was ready. And we can expect God to prune us many times at our different levels of growth. When we do bear fruit, He prunes us again so that we will bear even richer and more excellent fruit.

The process of pruning plants for future growth would be painful if plants had feelings, and since we as humans do have feelings, the process is painful for us. God deals with us in ways we wish He wouldn't. He cuts things out of our life that we would like to hang on to. He often removes people that are hindering or holding us back from His will for us. Sometimes we don't understand what He is doing, but I have learned over the years that it always turns out well in the end if I relax and let Him do what He wants to do. God always gets His way in the end, and wrestling with Him only makes the process take longer and actually makes it more painful.

The beginning of the Scripture passage that tells us that we can be like a tree firmly planted by the rivers of water, a tree that brings forth fruit in season and a tree that always prospers, is an example of the Word giving us specific direction in how to reach a higher level of maturity. It tells us not to follow ungodly counsel nor place ourselves in situations where we will be influenced by sinners or scornful people.[5] When we delight in spending our time learning and following the directives God gives in His Word, we will grow into new levels of maturity.

God is everything that He wants us to be. And when we receive Jesus into our hearts at the new birth, we receive the incorruptible Seed Himself.[6] We receive a seed, the Seed, in us of everything that

God is. The Seed of God comes to live on the inside of us. With watering, nurturing and proper care, the Seed in us will grow us into a great fruit-bearing plant.

How do we water and nurture the seed? By reading and meditating on God's Word, by seeking God and praying, by habitually applying what we learn and by keeping our focus on what is important.

Learn how to develop the fruit; do the best you can and don't expect to be perfect. Ask forgiveness when you need to;[7] receive it instead of dwelling on what you did wrong, and simply believe that God will do what His Word says He will do. You will have plenty of fruit in reserve for when you need it.

PART 2

DEVELOPING THE FRUIT

CHAPTER 7

LOVE — YOU HAVE IT IN YOU

There are many Christians who want to love with God's love, but in many cases, they don't know how. I am writing from experience. I could not love others because I had never received God's love for me. For many years I mentally acknowledged the Bible teaching that God loved me, but it was not a reality in my heart. Many Christians experience this. The first step in loving others with God's love is to seek to receive the reality that He loves us.

RECEIVE GOD'S LOVE, THEN GIVE IT AWAY

If we are Christians, if we have received Jesus, God's love is already in us for us to receive ourselves and give to others. The Bible tells us, *. . . the love of God is shed abroad in our hearts by the Holy Ghost which is given unto us.*[1] Already in us is the ability to love people.

As you begin to receive God's love and love yourself in a balanced way, God's love will begin to heal you emotionally so that you are not insecure and fearful or have a poor self-image. We need to spend a certain period of time in our life to settle those areas.

> LOVE WITH GOD'S LOVE BY FIRST RECEIVING THE REALITY THAT HE LOVES YOU.

Then instead of spending our entire life trying to receive healing from the pain of our childhood or other stages in our life, we need to go on. Someone reading this may be thinking, Joyce, **you don't know what I'm going through. My husband just left me with three kids. You don't know how I feel.**

Yes, I do know how you feel. I was sexually abused as a child, and I was abandoned by my first husband. He went to live two blocks from my house with another woman while I was pregnant with his child. I had to drive by his house every morning on my way to work carrying his child and knowing he was living with that woman. I know what it's like to hurt. But I also know what it's like to be healed. Almost everybody has been hurt — rejected, abused, treated badly in some way. I care about the emotionally hurt. I am very grateful to God for the emotional healing I have received, and teaching and ministering on emotional healing is a major part of my ministry. But God has put gifts in us that He wants us to use, and He wants us to receive His love, His healing and give His love to others rather than just sit around and bleed all our life.

Someone who is wounded doesn't just sit there and bleed. The person does something to stop the blood and clean out the wound so that it will heal. Then the person moves on. Some people may need a year or two, even three, to get their emotional wounds healed so they can move on. Some people may even need five. But they don't need twenty, thirty or forty years to receive healing.

If you don't receive healing from past emotional wounds, you never become strong enough to deal with fresh wounds that may come your way. I would like to promise you that you can reach a place where you will never get hurt again, but I cannot make that promise, and neither can anyone else. I can, however, promise you that Jesus the Healer is always available to heal every wound, old and new. If you never receive healing, the old wound keeps opening up and bleeding if someone hurts your feelings, and the love that God has put in you can never be released to bless others.

When that love of God that is in you heals you, you will find it easy to get along with people. You will see that people whom you might have had trouble getting along with in the past are no better or worse than anybody else. Because you like yourself, instead of getting your feelings hurt, you can shake off something that might have offended you and go on. When you receive God's love, you are so grateful for what He has done in your life, you are ready to let His love start to flow through you to the unlovely, the obnoxious, the people who are just the same way we used to be before God reached us.

Once, Dave was going through a transition, and for a brief period of time, acted very unlike the way he usually acts. I didn't think he was talking to me very nicely — he was a little grouchy and short. I tried to correct him a couple of times, and he said, "I'm not doing anything wrong — you're just too sensitive."

I said to the Lord, "This is not right. Dave is not talking to me right." Do you know what God's answer to me was? "How many years did you not talk to Dave right?" God was showing me that Dave was going through a challenging time in his own life, which Dave wouldn't have told me about. He is not the type to talk about something he is going through. Openly discussing inner feelings is usually easier for women than men.

Another time, a few years ago, I said to Dave, "All of our conversations are so shallow. We talk about all these little light things. I want to know about the deeper things in you."

He looked at me and said, "Joyce, this is as deep as I get."

If I want to talk about deep things, I need to talk with somebody other than Dave! But if I sit around talking about deep things with someone, I can also start overanalyzing everything and become confused! Most of the time life could be much simpler than we make it.

Receiving and expressing love is very important because without it, the Bible tells us that we are *nothing (a useless nobody)*.[2] We can help people with the gifts — we can *speak with the tongues of men and of angels*, but if we *do not have love*, we *have become a noisy gong or a clanging cymbal*.[3] We can operate in *the gift of prophecy*; we can *know all mysteries and all knowledge*; we can *have all faith* — enough to *remove mountains* — but if we *do not have love, we are nothing*.[4]

Even when we operate in great gifts, but without God's love, *the fruit of the Spirit*, which the other fruit express, we are nothing but a big noise or someone who isn't doing anybody any good! Many people in the body of Christ could say, "I am nothing but a loud noise." We can see from this particular description in the Bible just how important it is to develop the fruit of love in our lives. And if we concentrate on loving people, all the other fruit will come along as part of the package.

Instead of trying so hard to be perfect and please God, spend that time and effort with God expressing your love to Him. Just go through the day loving Him and letting Him love you. You will be surprised how much your behavior will improve.

LOVE IS ACTION

The Bible says that love is not theory or talk, but deeds.[5] Love is action, doing what needs to be done in every situation. Developing love isn't a horrible struggle; it is simply being good to people.

Start examining your life and seeking God more about your love walk — about your attitude, your thought life, what you say, how you treat people. How kind are you to people? What are you doing for people? How are you treating people who aren't treating you very nicely? Change your direction if you haven't been spending enough time focusing on how you act and sound, how you treat people, what you do for others and your expression of God's love to them through joy, peace, patience, goodness and kindness.

> CONCENTRATE ON LOVING PEOPLE, AND ALL THE OTHER FRUIT WILL COME ALONG.

We are known by our fruit, not only as individual members of the body, but corporately as churches, ministries and organizations. How we handle ourselves among the unbelievers is very important. A few years ago our ministry had, from what we were told, an unprecedented opportunity to put one of my books and a couple of other gifts like soap and shampoo into the hands of every single prisoner in the entire state of Missouri — 25,000 prisoners in seventeen different prisons. Obviously, we wanted to put the book into their hands. We weren't as concerned about the soap and the shampoo, but we were to give those in order to give them the book.

We wanted to do this; we had permission and were receiving the message that if this went well in the Missouri prisons, we would probably receive a similar opportunity in other states. And we are now doing this in other states as well and hope to do it all over the country.

We discovered that we had no comprehension of the time it would take to put the items into 25,000 bags. The first night our ministry people and their volunteers met to assemble the items, they realized that they would not come close to finishing. They called the office and asked for volunteers. The people in our office were so wonderful — after working all day, for two or three nights they went to the warehouse and assembled the bags, some working until ten, eleven, even midnight.

Dave and I went to the warehouse and saw that the people were having fun, really enjoying themselves. We need to simply give ourselves over to little things when opportunities arise. It doesn't always need to be some huge thing.

> WE CAN SHOW LOVE BY SIMPLY GIVING OURSELVES OVER TO LITTLE OPPORTUNITIES THAT ARISE.

After the bags were assembled, our volunteers delivered the items to the prisons. The group had a highly organized plan to get up at four or five in the morning to travel to the seventeen prisons. And after doing all the work of assembling the bags, they didn't just dump the bags at the prisons. In every prison that would allow them, they went from cell to cell, handing the books, shampoo, soap and a letter from our ministry to the prisoners and telling them, "God loves you. Jesus cares about you. We care about you."

Some of the prisoners sent us remarkable responses, which show how God's love in action can affect people.

One prisoner wrote:

> I'm a convict at the Tipton Correctional Center, and today the Christmas package was distributed. Among the usual assortment of sweets, there was your book, soap and shampoo. I'm normally not too impressed with people who well wish only once per year.

Many prisoners bring up the point that they feel as though the only time somebody cares if they're poor and hungry and needy is at Christmas when they are there in that condition all year.

The letter continued:

But your obvious care and concern by offering your inspirational story as well as some necessary items more than show me that you are coming truly from your heart. For what it's worth, I'm a heathen and do not believe in God, Satan or anything else. But I wanted you to know that your concern touched me deeply. And I think it is wonderful that people like you are still in the world.

I've spent the last twenty-one years in and out of this penitentiary, mostly in. And this is the first time that I can recall any religious organization providing the prison's entire population, perhaps the entire department of correction, with useful and costly gifts for Christmas.

This is an era when organized religious groups have made me so cynical due to either their political agendas or their leaders' less than admirable behavior themselves. Or their leaders are saying something but not living it because when they come in here, it's for some political agenda. They're really just wanting to look some certain way and there's really nothing behind it.

These prisoners spot phony fig trees quickly because they don't have much else to do but figure people out. And they probably become really good at judging character because if they didn't, they might not stay alive too long.

Your selfless generosity came as a pleasant surprise and forced me to reassess my views pertaining to ministers. Any ministry that donates so significantly to prisoners who are not in favor with many people these days, surely must truly be about God's ways. I am not a Christian and admittedly doubt that I will ever be one. But I do recognize and sincerely appreciate human decency, such as you folks have demonstrated with your generosity, compassion and work.

Prisons, as you may realize, have become fairly stark and harsh environments over the last decades or so due to self-serving. . . . I cannot adequately convey to you the sense of happiness and excitement the unexpected passing-out of gifts instilled within the entire prison. Your gifts noticeably made people feel better, not simply because we received material gifts, but due to the realization which accompanied the gifts that there are decent folks out there who do not despise us but thought of us at this time of year. Your gifts will go a long way toward tempering my cynicism and resentment regarding folks out there once I'm free again.

We've prayed for this prisoner's salvation at my ministry, so we expect to hear from him again that he has received the Lord. But look at what brought this about. All those volunteers sat in an empty, cold warehouse and did what some people might think was a job that wouldn't have much effect — putting soap, shampoo and a book in a plastic bag, instead of having their night off and getting their normal amount of sleep. What those volunteers were really doing was showing the fruit of the Spirit to people who would not believe what we said to them unless we showed them something real.

Here is another letter we received from a prisoner:

Hello, from Jefferson City Correctional Center, and I wish you a very Merry Christmas. I wanted to send this letter and thank you all for your act of kindness, generosity and love. So rare is it that a ministry group will take the time to share the Word of God with a bunch of convicts. Even more rare are the ones that will go beyond sharing the Word and show how true Christians show God's love to those around them.

I've seen many groups come into this prison and then walk out the door, thinking that their job is done. Just by showing up, you have done more in this one single act to show God's love to the men behind these walls than a dozen other combined ministries have done.

Sometimes we need to do a little more than just show up. Today many people really don't want to become involved with something because once we start involving ourselves with people, there are some expectations placed on us. People may want us to do something that we may not want to do; then we are not able to do what we want to do all the time.

The prisoner's letter continued:

This commitment, I know, had to cost you a lot, but it touched many lives with your one single act of kindness. You came to show God's love with your act of kindness.

This man recognized the fruit of the Spirit probably without knowing what it is.

There is a term used by the convicts here that says everything I want to say, and that term is "be what you're about." This means, if you say you're going to do something, then do it. If you're not a man of your word in prison, then you're nothing.

When a Christian group comes in here and preaches about showing the love of God in everything you do, and then they just walk away, they show these guys in here that the words that they have just heard are just that, words. You have shown them that there are people that not only talk His Word, but carry out His Words in their lives and their actions. And when they say that God loves them, they show it also. To give you an example of the effect that your actions had on the men here, let me explain a little bit of how our life is here.

Daily life behind these prison walls consists of anger, pain, torment and hostile acts. You hear guys scream just to get attention. You see them cuss, throw fits, and berate those around them just to make themselves feel like that they have some worth. There are times when the sound level gets so bad in this housing unit that a gun could go off, and you couldn't even hear it. But last night, after the institution passed out your care packages, it got so quiet that you could almost hear the pages of your book being turned.

I could feel a peace that I have never felt before behind these prison walls, settle down in the hearts of these men who've spent a lifetime trying to harden their hearts so that they couldn't feel the pain that they have always felt.

What happened was that all of a sudden every cell was full of the Word. Every cell had a book in there about how to apply the Word to your life — practical teaching: *Battlefield of the Mind, If Not for the Grace of God, Root of Rejection, Beauty for Ashes* or *"Me And My Big Mouth!"*

One letter came from a prisoner who said:

Your book, in the three days it took me to read it, did more for me than years of psychiatrists, psychologists, counseling, and everybody talking to me. . . .

People have got to have the Word!

This morning, when I went to chow hall, I saw more smiles on people's faces than I have ever seen since I've been here. To say that your act of love had touched so many men in here would be a total understatement.

My husband, my son David and my daughter Sandra went with some other people to the maximum-security area where people are on death row. They could look at the prisoners only through little slots where they gave them the book with the other items. Sandra said, "This one man looked out at me. The pain and the hopelessness in his eyes were just unbelievable. We prayed with him and told him that God loved him and that God cared about him."

> GOD'S WORD THROUGH A BOOK DID MORE IN THREE DAYS THAN YEARS OF PSYCHIATRIC AND PSYCHOLOGICAL COUNSELING.

Who knows what kind of a lifeline that may have been to him. There are many powerful ministries besides the ones seen on the platform in the pulpit. Our people who go to the prisons may meet at the office at 6:00 A.M. four times a week to begin driving to the prisons. And they are doing a powerful work. When we show the fruit, God will use our gifts.

We need to simply get about the business of showing God's love. Show it not only in the church, but start in your home. Sometimes the people we treat the worst are the ones who we know can't get away from us — the people we think have to put up with it. This is one reason why so many marriages are failing today — sooner or later people become fed up with that type of treatment and don't want to put up with it anymore.

WALKING IN THE MORE EXCELLENT WAY WITH AN EXCELLENT SPIRIT

As we have seen, the Bible tells us that love is the more excellent way. Paul said, *And this I pray: that your love may abound. . . .*[6] When we think of something abounding, we think of it meaning to grow and become so big that it chases people down, overtaking and overwhelming them. And Paul prayed this for the church. In the next verse he said, *So that you may surely learn to sense what is vital, and approve and prize what is excellent and of real value . . .*[7] that you may learn to choose and prize what is excellent, of real importance, and that you may learn to tell the difference.

To abound in love is the most excellent thing we can do. And we must do everything with an excellent spirit. We can't be an excellent person and not walk in love, and we can't walk in love and not be an excellent person. How can we say that we are walking in love if we are not treating people excellently?

If I'm a mediocre person, then I'm going to treat people in a mediocre way. It is very important to be a person of excellence — to

TO ABOUND IN LOVE IS THE MOST EXCELLENT THING WE CAN DO.

do our very best every day in all that we believe God is asking us to do, to always do every job to the best of our ability. The Bible tells us that Daniel was a man of excellence. Because of Daniel's excellent spirit, the king wanted to promote him.[8]

The good news is that God is not expecting us to give anything to anybody that He hasn't given us. How could God expect us to love people who are unlovely unless He equips us to be able to do that? And the more we use the fruit of the Spirit by being in situations that require us to use it, the more it grows.

CHAPTER 8

FAITHFULNESS —
NEVER GIVING UP

One of the most important lessons we can learn is to be faithful with something until God lets us know that we are finished with it. There are times when God will call us out of one place and put us into another one — no doubt about that. But I don't believe that God changes the plan very frequently.

When Dave and I found the church we have attended for twenty years, Life Christian Church, it was brand new, with only about thirty people attending. I knew it was where God wanted me to be because I really sensed the anointing in a very strong way. And almost immediately there was some kind of divine connection between our pastor, Rick, and his wife, Donna, with Dave and me. We have been committed to the relationship for over twenty years now.

The relationship hasn't always been easy, especially for Rick and Donna when working with me. Next to my husband, the other members of the body God used to help me grow up and clean up my messes were Rick and Donna. Rick told me a long time ago, "Joyce, you and I are mouths in the body of Christ. You are a mouth." That is true because my gift is communication. But back in those days when my fruit was so immature, I really was a mouth. Not only did all my gifts come out my mouth, but in keeping with the Scripture, . . . *For out of the abundance of the heart the mouth speaks,*[1] I got myself in a lot of trouble by all the other things I let come out of it. But because of our faithfulness to stay committed to the relationship, we have seen tremendous fruit come out of it.

A faithful person knows what God has put in their heart, and even though many times they feel like quitting, they don't give up. They don't leave a place because they want to leave, or a job because they don't want to be there anymore. They don't get out of a relationship because they don't want to bother with certain things in it anymore. A faithful person is committed to doing whatever God tells them to do no matter what it costs them personally.

COMMITMENT TO GOD'S PLAN

A faithful person sees something all the way through to the end. There are so many divorces and so much job-hopping and church-hopping in society today because many people don't understand what commitment means. Years ago people did not hop around from church to church as they do today. They understood that no matter where they went, they wouldn't like everything that would happen. We might as well go somewhere and stay there. The way we grow is to stick with something.

The world needs to see stability and faithfulness in us. God impressed upon me one time, "I have got My people strategically placed everywhere — everywhere." I realized that the whole world is not full of people who don't love God, as we often think. I clearly saw that many believers are out there, but many times we cannot tell who they are. God is waiting for us to mature and consistently show forth the fruit of His Spirit so we will be recognized for who and what we are. There are many people with deep needs in our society, and Christians should be prepared to give them answers that will help them. However, many believers in Jesus Christ just want to preach to people, but they don't want to consistently display the fruit of the Spirit, which is the true evidence of our Christianity.

> THE WAY WE GROW IS TO STICK WITH SOMETHING.

The Bible says that we are to be salt and light.[2] Jesus is the light of the world[3] and we are to let people see His light of life in us.

We probably all know people we are happy to see when they walk into a room. Christians who let their light shine can change the atmosphere in a room when they walk in. Unbelievers ought to feel as though a light is coming on when we walk in the door even though they don't really understand what is happening. They can reach the point of being happy to see us because everybody in the whole place feels better when we walk in. When you arrive at your job in the morning, it ought to feel as though even the whole atmosphere lightens up a level. People will look forward to your being around. We need to be the way Jesus is if we want to show Him to people.

When people realize that we are Christians, they start reading us first to decide whether they are interested in ever reading the Bible. God is making His appeal to the world through us.[4] The biggest majority of people watching us have probably tried religion (as opposed to a relationship with Jesus) and had a bad experience. So whatever we do or wherever we go — if we get our nails done in a place where there aren't any other Christians, at our job, at the doctor or dentist, every time we walk in the door — people ought to be glad to see us coming. And when they begin watching us, they will begin seeing the characteristics of the way God wants us to live, even if they didn't learn those characteristics growing up. Jesus' light in us will draw them; the fruit and salt in us will make them hungry and thirsty for what we have. We should be careful, however, not to try to appear overly religious (which is usually obnoxious), pushing at everybody our fourteen translations of the Bible. Sometimes we need to just keep our Bibles and our tracts in our pockets until we show people some good fruit.

The fruit of faithfulness is listed as *faith* in the *King James Version*, but many Bible translations call this fruit *faithfulness*.

God is faithful (reliable, trustworthy, and therefore ever true to His promise, and He can be depended on). . . .[5]

God is everything that He wants us to be. He can expect us to be faithful because He has put a seed of that fruit of faithfulness on the inside of us. A faithful person is someone we can depend on — someone who shows up where they say they will be at the time they say they will be there, someone whom you can count on to do something they say they will do for you. It is wonderful to have friends that you can depend on. Have you ever had a few friends that even though you love them, you can't depend on them? That gets old, doesn't it? We want to be able to depend on people.

To be faithful, we cannot let ourselves be led by our feelings. We have to go deeper than that carnal, shallow level of doing what we feel, think or want. To be Christlike, we must be faithful to not quit until we have finished doing what God has given us to do. We need to decide that in whatever He has assigned us to do, we will cross that finish line.

CHECK WITH GOD BEFORE YOU LEAVE

God never gives up on us, and we should never give up. We especially shouldn't be the kind of people that give up on something because it is hard. If God's anointing and blessing lifts off something because He is finished with it, that is the time to stop doing it — but not before. There are times when God will call you out of one place to put you in another one. But in that case we really need to make sure that God is finished and that it is not our flesh that doesn't want to press through to the end.

> DON'T QUIT UNTIL YOU HAVE FINISHED DOING WHAT GOD HAS GIVEN YOU TO DO.

Some decisions are minor ones, but some decisions are ones that we are meant to stay with for our lifetime. I believe that we should look at the decision we make to attend a particular church as a long-term decision. Dave and I have left a few churches. One time we moved; another time the church folded up; the other time they asked me to leave because they didn't agree with my theology after I became Spirit filled!

I don't believe that God changes His mind very often about where we should attend church. I believe that God wants us to be planted in a body of believers who will help us grow up. He wants our gifts to flourish and blossom there, and after we have drawn and learned from others, He wants us to turn around and be of benefit to people who come in just as other people there helped us grow.

I also believe that we don't need to find a new ministry to function in every three or four days or months. It is true that sometimes we need to step out in faith and do a few different things before we settle in to the right place. But some people feel that they are called to work in the nursery until they have to change a couple of dirty diapers. Then all of a sudden, they believe that their calling has changed to be on the worship team until the choir director calls a practice on a night of the week when they don't want to attend. Then their calling changes to being an usher. But on some cold night when they are assigned to the parking lot, they suddenly believe that they are called to something else. It's amazing how many people don't want to do the hard part of the job, but every job has a hard part that needs to be done.

APPRECIATE THE FAITHFUL PEOPLE IN YOUR LIFE

I know many faithful people. For example, two very faithful people in our church who were wallpapering our house, went home to clean up in order to arrive at the church in plenty of time to do their job there, as they did every night of the meeting schedule. When our church has a series of week-long meetings, and these two people are involved in our conferences, they are always faithfully there to usher or do whatever else they have committed to do, meeting after meeting, conference after conference. It isn't always fun to work meetings every single night for a week. Their bodies get tired just like everybody else's, and they feel it too when they get up and go to work the next day. But they are faithful, faithful people.

My husband is not on the platform in meetings as I am most of the time, so he isn't as visible, but he is an example of a faithful man. He is a faithful friend, husband and father; he is faithful in his responsibilities at the ministry.

Dave was confirmed in a denominational church that gives each person a Scripture when they are confirmed. It is supposed to be a lifetime Scripture, one that will be important throughout their life. He received as his Scripture Revelation 2:10: . . . *be thou faithful unto death, and I will give thee a crown of life* (KJV).

The word *faithful*[6] is defined as, "Firm in adherence to the truth and to the duties of religion." In the dictionary that I'm using, Noah Webster's 1828 *American Dictionary of the English Language,* a Scripture is inserted after almost every definition. And the Scripture that follows this definition of *faithful* is, "Be thou *faithful* unto death, and I will give thee a crown of life. Rev. ii," — the lifetime Scripture Dave was given when he was confirmed!

Since this dictionary is based on the Word of God, we can understand the word "religion" to mean "relationship with God." To have a right relationship with anybody, there are certain duties involved with that relationship, certain things that we need to do to keep the relationship healthy. In the same way we need to be faithful to the duties of our relationship with God. We need to be faithful to God in prayer, in our Bible study, in worship and in church attendance.

The definition of *faithful* continues: "2. Firmly adhering to duty. . . loyal. . . . 3. Constant in the performance of duties or services; exact in attending to commands; as a *faithful* servant."

This last part of the definition means to be exact in attending to what an authority gives us to do. In other words, when a boss, a pastor, parents, a husband or other authority gives us an instruction, as a faithful person we are to do exactly what we have been asked to do. Some people do a little of what they are asked to do and a little bit of what they want to do. If you as an employer or other authority have experienced people fulfilling your instructions this way, you know how aggravating it is. You ask the person to do something and, because they don't think that what you told them to do was exactly right, they will change it just a little bit. They think they have an idea that will make it better. Then you end up with a result that won't accomplish the purpose that you wanted in the first place. I so much appreciate the people that just do what I ask them to do.

In the First Book of Samuel, the Bible gives us an example of someone who had a problem with not following God's instructions exactly. Saul, whom God promoted to become the first king of Israel, had a problem in his heart. When God asked Saul to do something, Saul did 75 or 80 percent of what God asked him to do, but always did a little bit of what he wanted to do. As a result, the Lord finally rejected him from being king over Israel.

The 1828 version of Webster includes in its definition of *faithful* the examples:

"4. . . . A government should be *faithful* to its treaties; individuals, to their word."

"6. True to the marriage covenant; as a *faithful* wife or husband."

"8. Constant; not fickle; as a *faithful* lover or friend."

And another example that is followed with a reference to Scripture:

"9. True; worthy of belief. 2. Tim. ii."

It is so valuable to have people in our life that we can believe in. A few years ago I started having some blood pressure problems that were pretty severe for a while, which has since been taken care of. When I started having the blood pressure problems, I was committed to holding several months of conferences. At that time I was holding three, even four, a month. I never knew exactly how I was going to feel.

Until I was through the crisis time, which was a couple of months, I had a friend who, although he was busy pastoring a church, went to our conferences with us and just sat there just in case I needed him. He might receive the offering or come up and give an exhortation. Many times he didn't even preach. Or, sometimes he would preach in one of the morning sessions, and I would preach in all the other sessions. When someone is willing to do something like that for you, that is faithfulness.

When we have a faithful friend like that, we need to appreciate them. We need to really appreciate all the people in our life who have been faithful.

> HAVING PEOPLE IN YOUR LIFE YOU CAN BELIEVE IN IS SO VALUABLE.

According to Webster's 1828 dictionary, the word *faithfully* [7] means to behave "In a faithful manner; with good faith. 2. With strict adherence to allegiance and duty. . . . 3. With strict observance of promises, vows, covenants or duties; without failure of performance; honestly; exactly. . . . 4. Sincerely; with strong assurances. . . ."

It is important for the tendency among many Christians who haven't developed the fruit of faithfulness to get back to being faithful in everything they do. For some people, simply doing what they tell people they are going to do, no matter how they feel, would be great progress.

If you want to be used by God, or if you are being used by God and want to be used by God in a greater way, then always remember this: **God only promotes faithful men and women.** God promotes those who have proven themselves to be faithful. Then, when you prove yourself to be faithful in one area or level, God will promote you to another level.

COMMITMENT, THE SAFETY NET

Learning about faithfulness and commitment is one of the most important things you can ever do. Commitment is what we need. Commitment is a safety net for us. It keeps us doing the things that we need to do even when we don't feel like doing them. If we know that we're committed to someone to do something, we will often do it if for no other reason than just to save face.

> GOD PROMOTES PEOPLE WHO HAVE PROVEN THEMSELVES TO BE FAITHFUL.

There are many people who want to be promoted, but they don't want to be faithful. And many people who aren't promoted in their timing run off to another place to see if they will be promoted there. Sometimes in our ministry we watch people with strong gifts and talents whom we are planning to promote into leadership or management. But, a few months before they would receive a promotion or a raise that they have been believing for, they decide to run off somewhere else where they think they will find what they want. I find that to be very disturbing and sad, really. Many plans have been thwarted because of a lack of faithfulness; there must be many people in the body of Christ who are trying to find their way but have never stayed in one place long enough to find it.

WHEN GOD IS READY TO PROMOTE YOU, NO ONE CAN STOP HIM

Again, it is so important not to leave a place unless you are sure that God wants you to leave. You may want to leave because you are experiencing unpleasant circumstances; but realize, God may be testing you. If you are mad at the leader, realize that God may be purifying your heart and testing you before He moves you to the next level. One thing that you can be assured of is that when you are faithful to God and your position, when God is ready to promote you, no person or thing will be able to hold you back.

When God is ready to promote you, if the person that is in authority over you won't do what God is telling them to do, God will move you under someone who will listen to Him and do what He says. So if your gifts and talents aren't being used in the position you are in, be careful to watch your attitude to not become disgruntled. Wait to make sure that it is God Who is telling you to leave and not the devil trying to drive you out too early because he knows that you might miss a blessing that is right around the corner.

In my opinion, it is better to stay a bit too long than leave too soon. I stayed in my job at the church a whole year after God told me to leave, and I wasn't being willfully and knowingly disobedient. If I had left before God told me to leave, then it would have been one of the biggest mistakes of my life. I was about to step out into my own ministry. Before I did something like that, I had to be certain that God told me to do it. I had a good job there, and I already had a good ministry. I didn't want to become the town fool! So I said, "God, prove to me that You want me to do this."

After that year, I actually felt as though I was losing the anointing when I ministered. I remember in one of the early morning prayer meetings I said, "God, what is wrong with me?" He answered me, "Joyce, I told you a year ago to get out in your own ministry, and you're still here."

I stayed a little bit longer than I should have, but I'm glad that I did because when I did leave, there was no question in my mind that it was God telling me to leave. If you make a major decision to move into something different without knowing for certain that God told you to do it, you will wonder if you made the right move when you encounter attacks from Satan. You can get into confusion if everything is not coming together as fast as you thought it would. Then you will wonder the rest of your life if you did the right thing. Reading this could be life-changing for you if you are being tempted right now to move into something else that God isn't telling you to do, especially if you are thinking of going out into your own ministry or business.

When I worked for my church, my pastor believed for my paycheck. Now with my own ministry, I have over 450 people to believe in the money for their paychecks. And any flaws we might have when we're out there on our own show up really fast when we don't have anybody else to clean up our messes.

In Psalm 12:1 we read that David said, *Help, LORD! For principled and godly people are here no more; faithfulness and the faithful vanish from among the sons of men.* If David said that in his day, we ought to know that being faithful is as important today as it was then. Many leaders today know how hard it is to find people who will be really faithful, people who will stick with them when they find out their leader isn't perfect and has flaws, people who won't start strife. The Bible says, *A friend loves at all times, and is born, as a brother, for adversity.*[8] In other words a true friend is a person who is born to stick with you in your hard and not-so-nice times.

I believe that one of the saddest things in our society today is that we don't have this kind of loyalty and commitment. Many people miss out on so much because they aren't faithful to stay with something until God tells them to do something else. Even sadder is that most of them won't know what incredible blessings they missed.

Psalm 12 continues, *To his neighbor each one speaks words without use or worth or truth; with flattering lips and a double heart [deceitfully] they speak* (verse 2). We need single-minded men and women who can set their hearts on something and stick with it without being double-minded and speaking empty words, without planning to carry out what they say or changing their minds. They believe one thing one day and the next they don't. One day they like you and are for you and the next day they don't and aren't.

Dave and I will always stick with each other.

There are some people who work with Dave and me who I believe will be with us as long as we are in ministry.

There are many examples in the Bible of faithful people. Moses was faithful in all the house of God. That means he was faithful to do exactly the duties that God gave him to do day after day, month after month, year after year, even when he didn't feel like being faithful. Moses was so faithful that even when his sister and brother, Miriam and Aaron, spoke against him, he obviously loved them and remained faithful to them. He had so much faithfulness in him that even when the people in his life didn't do what was good for him, he remained the same way.

Moses was a man who had developed God's character. The Bible tells us that God remains faithful even when we are faithless.[9] That is the way God wants us to be. If everybody else is faithless, then we remain faithful. If you feel as though you are the only one who is being nice, the only one who apologizes or tries to do the right thing, keep on doing it. Keep bearing that fruit of faithfulness.

The Bible tells us about the many examples in Joseph's life of his great faithfulness. When Potiphar's wife tempted him, it had to have been extremely hard for him to resist. That woman spent a lot of time trying to lure him. Besides having the thought that he might be killed if he resisted her, he also had to deal with the temptation that as a young man he had to be going through in his flesh. He was a young man with emotions just like everybody else. But he was faithful to God and resisted that temptation even though it meant that he spent years in prison for something he didn't do. And because of Joseph's faithfulness, God not only brought him out of prison but moved him into a position to rule over Egypt under Pharaoh!

Charlotte — our Assistant General Manager who manages the phone, data processing, prayer and correspondence departments in our ministry — used to be so full of fear that she shook and cried when she tried to talk to me. When I tried to give her more responsibility she would say, "I don't know if I can do this."

One day I told her, "Charlotte, you've got to get over this. We don't have time to go through this all the time." As you are reading this you may be thinking, **That's really mean.** But Charlotte went home and talked with God about it and He told her, "It's time for you to grow up." She took action and she started changing. She got so good that we started promoting her. And recently out of our whole organization we chose six people to be division managers. We wanted faithful people who wouldn't leave after three or four months or a year after we put a great deal of time and effort into training them. We have many wonderful, faithful people whom I am so grateful to have, but we could only choose six division managers, and Charlotte was one of them.

I can almost guarantee that in order for you to grow, God will put someone in your life to correct you. The day that I corrected Charlotte, she could have gone home saying, "I don't have to put up

WHEN GOD PROMOTES YOU, NOTHING WILL BE ABLE TO HOLD YOU BACK.

with this. That woman is insensitive. She is hard and doesn't understand what I've been through and why I have all these fears." But instead she went home and she listened to God, not to her feelings. Many people simply need to grow up instead of being quitters and running away every time someone corrects them or they don't like the way things are going. Otherwise they won't have what it takes to be what God needs them to be.

The Bible tells us that Elisha was faithful to Elijah even though from what we read about Elijah, he may have been a stern man.

And when Elijah died, Elisha received a double portion of the anointing that was on Elijah's life. Some people need to stick around long enough to get some of the anointing of the people they are under.

Keep growing that fruit of faithfulness in whatever you do even though it won't always be easy. If you are faithful over little things, God will make you ruler over much.[10] And when the time comes and God promotes you, nobody will be able to hold you back. Being faithful will lead you into the type of exceptional life that God really wants you to have.

CHAPTER 9

GOODNESS — GOING ABOUT DOING GOOD

GOD IS GOOD

The fruit of goodness is based on the foundation that God is good and will manifest His goodness by instructing us in His way.[1] Therefore, if God instructs us in His ways, and He is good, then God must instruct me in how to be good myself, how to let His goodness flow through me. Learning to be good to people, no matter how difficult it may seem at times, is a basic requirement of experiencing God's goodness in life.

Have you ever noticed how excited we are about someone being good to us? We may say, "They are such a good person." Or, "He or she is so good to me." But when it comes to being good to someone else, we're not nearly as interested. It's time to get our minds off ourselves and say, "From now on, God, every day I'm going to be good to someone. In fact, every day, all day, I will be good to all people."

If you think about it, there are numerous ways to be good to people. People are starving for somebody — anybody — to show them the love of God. Demonstrating love starts with a simple act of goodness. To display God's character, you must make a choice to be good to people.

Start by asking God to develop the fruit of goodness inside of you. Ask God to put opportunities in your path that allow you daily to demonstrate goodness to someone. Ask God to display His character through you. To make someone feel better, give someone joy, make someone happy. Ask God to use you as an instrument to bless someone. You'll be amazed at how your life will change by simply getting your mind off yourself, **your** problem, **your** wants and **your** needs. Leave your list of "I wants" in God's hands. Instead, concentrate on being a blessing wherever you go. You'll be surprised at how many of the "I wants" on your list will be taken care of because of your goodness to others.

Let's go back to the basics. God is good. All the time.[2] The Bible says that God is good to the just and the unjust. The Bible also says that His goodness is laid up for those who fear, revere and worship Him: *Goodness which you have wrought for those who trust and take refuge in You before the sons of men!*[3]

Notice the term *before the sons of men*. That says to me that if I will not be a closet Christian, but be open and live my Christianity before the sons of men, God will store up His goodness for me. There are a number of people today who profess to be Christians but don't want to admit it or live it outside of their Christian circle. They're Sunday morning Christians, but on Monday morning you can't tell any difference between them and those who never claimed to be a Christian.

That was me twenty-two years ago when I'd been a Christian for years and I was on the church board, my husband was an elder in the church, our kids went to the Christian schools, our social life revolved around church and we had a set of Christian bumper stickers for each car — the whole nine yards. However, in my neighborhood, you couldn't tell the difference between my behavior and any other housewife on the block who wasn't saved. At work you couldn't tell any difference in what I said or did from any of my coworkers who weren't saved. Perhaps there was some difference, but not enough to notice. I was not taking a stand for God like I should have.

That's true for many of us. Because we're afraid of being rejected, or isolated or laughed at, we're afraid to take a stand and say, "I really don't want to hear a dirty joke. I'm a Christian and I don't want to hear any filthy language. I'm not really interested in going to an R-rated movie, or hitting the bars after work. That's not what I'm about. My life and my relationship with God are too important to me." That is what the Scripture means when it says, . . . *those who trust and take refuge in You before the sons of men!*

This eliminates lukewarm, compromising Christianity. Reading about the fruit of the Spirit, specifically goodness, will not do you any good unless you're ready to take a full, 100 percent stand for Christ.

GOD IS WAITING TO BE GOOD TO YOU

It is no accident that you are living at this time in church history. I firmly believe that God hand selected those He wanted living during the time when Jesus will return. I do not take lightly the responsibility that God has given me. With opportunity comes responsibility. It's time to stop compromising.

Only goodness and mercy shall follow you all the days of your life.[4] **Only.** Read this again. **Only** goodness and mercy are following you. Nothing bad, nothing negative. Only goodness and mercy. Goodness and mercy follow you everywhere you go. The two work hand in hand because God cannot be good to you without you receiving His mercy. We cannot **deserve** the goodness of God because as people we are not perfect and we make mistakes. So God's goodness to us requires His mercy.

> ONLY GOODNESS AND MERCY SHALL FOLLOW YOU ALL THE DAYS OF YOUR LIFE.

Even though we are not perfect and we make mistakes, we can at least take a strong stand for the Lord.

Moses said to the Lord in Exodus 33:13, *I pray You, If I have found favor in Your sight, show me now Your way. . . .* (AMP) or, *let me know Thy ways . . .* (NASB). Show me your ways. I love that. Many people just want to see the acts of God, but Moses wanted to see His ways. Teach me the ways, teach me Your ways, God. One of God's ways is goodness. The Scripture goes on to say, beginning in verse 18, *And Moses said, I beseech You, show me Your glory.* And God replied, *I will make all My goodness pass before you. . .* (verse 19).

That's such an awesome thought. To make all of My goodness pass before you. I believe God desires the same thing for all of us — for all His goodness to pass before us. God wants you to really understand how good He wants to be to you. God desires to pour His goodness out upon you.

But God also said, *You can not see My face, for no man shall see Me and live. . . . Behold, there is a place beside Me, and you shall stand upon the rock, And while My glory passes by, I will put you in the cleft of the rock and cover you with My hand until I have passed by. Then I will take away My hand and you shall see My back; but My face shall not be seen.*[5] I read that Scripture for a number of years without really understanding it. Then one day God suddenly gave me a revelation about those verses.

In essence He said, "I'm going to hide you in the cleft of the rock over here . . ." which I believe represents Jesus because we are hidden in Christ. He went on to say, "I'm going to pass by, and I will put My hand over you so you can't see My face." In other words, "You cannot see Me coming. Once I pass by, I'll remove my hand and you will be able to see Me from behind." My understanding of this passage is that as a Christian you can be in desperate trouble. Perhaps you've been waiting and waiting, and God has been moving toward you every second of each day with the answer. But you can't see Him coming. Remember we are hidden in Christ. Even though our need has not been met to our satisfaction, we're in Christ. Therefore, we're safe in that place. In Christ, there's a certain kind of provision for us. It may not be everything we want, but it keeps us. It helps us. It gives us what we need to get through the situation. As the Bible says in Psalm 91:15, God will be with us in trouble and deliver us. Many times before God delivers us **from** trouble, we have to be satisfied with Him being with us **in** trouble. We don't see God coming, but at all times He is moving toward us. You may not have yet seen the goodness of God manifest in your life, but keep in mind it's moving toward you.

GOD WILL WORK GOOD OUT OF BAD

When we first come to Christ, we are a mess. Our life is a tangle of bad relationships, wrong thoughts, financial disaster and numerous other calamities we've managed to get ourselves into. But God is so good that He untangles and overcomes all the bad in our life. But it takes time. For some, it took years to get into those messes, so it may take time to overcome the problems we've created. As God moves toward us, He's solving, and dealing with, and taking care of situations. All the time we're hidden in the Rock, in Christ.

Then God says, "I will pass by, and I will remove My hand, and although you won't see My face, you will see Me from behind." God is telling us that we will not see Him coming, but we will certainly know when He's been there.

Sometimes you can stick with something and you try this and try that and try something else and nothing is working. Of course the devil is right there saying, "God doesn't love you. He has no good plan for your life. God is being good to everybody except you. You must be in sin. You must be doing something wrong. You don't have any faith."

Those are just Satan's lies to fight off while you're waiting. Don't quit and give up on God. His goodness is moving toward you right now. You will see the goodness of God in your life. Who does God want to be good to but His children?

I'm always looking for something to do for my kids. Dave and I are in our fifties now, and we've raised four kids. By the time you reach our age, you're a little more stable financially. You're in a position to bless your children in a different way than what you could when they were little. We have four grown children. I'm always looking for something I can do for them. Anytime they say they like something if there's any way I can possibly do it, I'm going to get it for them. That is God's attitude toward His children who love Him.

You might think, **I wish I could do more for my children or friends, but I don't have the means to do it.**

Some people won't do anything if they can't do everything they want to do.

Start where you can. I began a long time ago. You must start somewhere to get to where you want to be. **God is good!** Exodus

34:6 says, *And the Lord passed by before him, and proclaimed, The Lord! the Lord! a God merciful and gracious, slow to anger, and abundant in loving-kindness and truth.* We need to believe, really **believe** in the goodness of God. Perhaps your belief in God's goodness is something that you've let slide to a back burner. God wants you to get your expecter out. Your expecter may be buried in a dusty closet somewhere. The only thing you are expecting is more trouble.

> WE NEED TO BELIEVE, REALLY **BELIEVE** IN THE GOODNESS OF GOD.

What happens when you have a chain of disappointments and discouraging events in your life? You get to the point where you start expecting trouble. Every once in a while, in any ministry and church, little attacks come along. One occurred in our ministry recently. Things have been flowing smoothly for a long time. The ministry hasn't had any problems. I preach against strife, so it's a real big issue for us to have any strife among the staff. But last week, two people were fired for being in strife.

Sometimes when God is getting ready to take you forward, He's got to get rid of a few little things here and there because they will be trouble when you advance to that next level. However, here's what happens. Because you've dealt with so much stuff, you dread to answer the phone, open the mail or step out and take a risk. That's what you've got to beware of. Be very careful that when several things happen in a row that weren't so good that you don't begin expecting only bad news to come your way.

Some of you may be in that place right now. You've been through a bunch of junk. You've been through trials. You've been attacked in your job and your finances. You've been attacked in your body and by people you thought were friends. You're almost in that mindset of, **What's going to happen next?** I don't care how long the trouble lasts. I don't care how long that child of yours acts out, you **expect** them to turn around and serve God. You **expect** the events in your life to turn for good.

My brother was gone from my life for fourteen years, living in sin, drugs and alcohol. Within the last few years he's been born again, baptized in the Holy Ghost and delivered from the addictions that plagued him. He's now working in the ministry on the maintenance crew. God can **suddenly** change people.

Suddenly a light showed around Paul on the Damascus road and he was saved.[6] **Suddenly.** The day before he was out collecting Christians so they could put them in jail.

You never know what may happen. God is very creative. Your husband may go out to get drunk tonight and suddenly fall off the barstool when Jesus appears to him. You say, "Well, what if I believe all that stuff that you're saying and nothing happens?" Well, I'll tell you. Even if you believe what you are reading here and nothing changes in your life, you'll still be happier. Because if you don't believe in something good, you will have a sour life. And sour people turn everything around them sour. I don't want to be around sour people who do nothing but complain about their problems. I want to hear what God can do, what God has done. I want to hear your expectations for what God will do in your life.

Are you expecting something good to happen to you? [*What, what would have become of me*] *had I not believed that I would see the Lord's goodness in the land of the living!*[7] David said, "What in the world would have happened to me? What kind of condition would I be in? What pit would I be in had I not believed that I would see the Lord's goodness, not in heaven, but in the land of the living."

We spend a lot of time talking about the way it will be in heaven. I'm here right now. I want to know something good is going to happen to me **now**. I'm looking forward to heaven, but I don't believe that God put us here to try and muddle through till we get to heaven so we can finally have some joy. John 10:10 says, *The thief comes only in order to steal and kill and destroy. I [Jesus] came that they [meaning us] may have and enjoy life, and have it in abundance (to the full, till it overflows).* One of the greatest curses we can come under is to live a life that we never enjoy.

I'm going to enjoy my life. I'm going to have so much fun, I'm going to drive the devil nuts. You'd better surround yourself with a few Christians who encourage you during attacks. Surround yourself with some strong men and women of God. Don't seek out four or five negative people and just sit around and be negative together. Not only is that unproductive, it's boring. Find someone that will edify and exhort and give you the Word and tell you, "Cheer up, c'mon." No wonder you have problems if all you have is a bunch of friends who complain. Those spirits of pessimism and depression are transferable.

What would have become of me, David said, had I not **believed** that I would see the Lord's goodness in the land of the living? Just because something happens that appears to be a dead end to you, doesn't mean it is a dead end.

If God closes a door, He opens a window. If Satan seals up every door and every window, God will yank the roof off. We serve a God Who makes a way where there doesn't seem to be a way.

He's the Waymaker. Jesus said, *I am the way, the truth, and the life. . . .*[8] Wait and hope for and expect the Lord. Be brave and of good courage and let your heart be stout and enduring. Wait for and hope for and expect the Lord. Many people are depressed because they don't believe that anything good can happen to them. I defy you to stay depressed while believing that God's goodness is going to manifest in your life. You can't do it. As soon as you start believing something good is going to happen, that spirit of depression will leave.

If you are clinically depressed, something is affecting your body and needs to be attended to physically. That is one type of depression that stems from a physical cause. However, there's so much emotional depression that stems from the way people think and talk. Did you know that you can become depressed by the words you say? Start talking about the goodness of God. Just start thinking about and talking about the goodness of God and what all God can do in your life. Each morning, before you get out of bed, before you get in the shower, repeat ten times, "I believe something good is going to happen to me today." The goodness of God will begin to manifest in your life. Remember, **God is good.** Tell God, "If You're looking for somebody to be good to today, here I am!"

> GOD MAKES A WAY WHERE THERE DOESN'T SEEM TO BE A WAY.

Begin to **aggressively** believe for the goodness of God. This should not be some little passive thing that you tuck in the back of your brain somewhere. We get real good at this in the Church. "Jesus loves me; this I know, for the Bible tells me so."

However, as soon as trouble arrives, you begin to cry, "Well, God, don't You love me anymore?" You must aggressively believe these things. You must take a stand and say, "I believe in the goodness of God." Just think how much better you'll feel if you begin to think and talk about the good things that God has done in your life. Isaiah 30:18, in *The Amplified Bible,* says, *And therefore the Lord [earnestly] waits [expecting, looking and longing] to be gracious to you. . . .* That simply means to be good to you.

God is actually waiting, looking, longing, trying to get an entrance into your life, just as I look for ways to be good to my kids.

If I can do that as a human being, with my problems and the things my flesh wants to do; if I can want to be good to my friends or want to be good to my kids, then you can too! Dave and I have a good friend that loves pretty ties. When Dave and I are out shopping and we see ties, I can't tell you how many times we say, "Oh, Don would like that one." We may find a tie that Dave really likes and say, "Let's get two of them and send one to Don." If I can do that for a friend that I only see a few times a year, what can I expect God to do in my life? Any inkling of wanting to be good to somebody came from God's Spirit being in us. If I can want to be good to somebody, how much more does God want to be good to me? I'm not good to my kids because they're perfect. I'm not good to my friends because they're perfect friends. I simply enjoy being good to people. I have discovered that it's much more fun to be good to somebody than to be mean. I frankly got tired of being unhappy.

I learned that I could make myself happy by being good to somebody. I believe that part of God's joy is in His goodness, His joy, His inherent joy that's in Him. Jesus prayed that we would have His joy filling our souls. In John 17:13 Jesus prayed, *And now I am coming to You: I say these things while I am still in the world, so that My joy may be made full and complete and perfect in them [that they may experience My delight fulfilled in them, that My enjoyment may be perfected in their own souls, that they may have My gladness within them, filling their hearts].* He was praying that we would have His joy filling and diffusing our souls — His gladness, His joy. He said, . . . *My peace I give to you. . . .*[9] Part of that joy comes from just wanting to be good.

The Bible says in the Psalms that angels harken to the voice of God's Word.[10] We speak the Word of God out of our mouth and say, "God is good. I'm expecting You, based on Isaiah 30:18,[11] to be good to me." You'd better watch out because angels start moving in your direction with blessing. And you know, it may not happen overnight. If you've got a long, negative pattern in your life, you will have to override that. You may be tested.

This doesn't mean you'll never have a trial, or that you'll never have any trouble. However, in the midst of trouble, keep saying, "God is good. God is good. God is good." In 1989 I was attacked with breast cancer. I went in for a routine checkup and suddenly, overnight, I was in the hospital having surgery. Cancer is a scary word. It brings up all kinds of emotions. I had to wait for test results.

During that period of waiting, God said, "There's a few affirmations I want you to keep in your mouth during this period." One of those was, "God is good. God is good." He said, "I want to hear you repeating that constantly. 'God is good. God is good.'"

That needs to stay in front of us because even when you have problems, even when you have trouble, when you have disappointments, when things happen in a different way than you thought or a different way than what you planned, the goodness of God doesn't change.

God's goodness certainly did manifest in my life. Although I did need surgery, the cancer had been discovered before it had a chance to invade my lymph nodes; therefore, I did not need radiation or chemotherapy. Some people only look at what went wrong, but I believe we should look at what could have gone wrong had God's goodness not interrupted the problem.

Joseph had a few interruptions in his life. He was whiling away the hours being a dreamer, just dreaming the dreams of God. Because he had a dream and his father loved him and gave him a pretty coat, his brothers hated him. They were jealous.[12] Yes, Joseph probably used a lack of wisdom in telling his brothers his dream. He probably could have used more wisdom to prepare him for what

God had for him to do. But he basically was just a sweet guy who needed to grow up. However, his brothers hated him. And Joseph spent years in prison for something he didn't do. But in the end he said, "What you meant for my harm, God intended for my good."[13]

We serve a God Who is so good, He even takes what the devil meant for harm and works something for good. God has taken some awful things in my life and worked them for good. *And we know that God causes all things to work together for good to those who love God, to those who are called according to His purpose.*[14]

All things! Everything . . . every trial, every tribulation, every person who comes against you. When I was baptized in the Spirit, my friends came against me. I lost all my friends because they didn't believe in the baptism of the Holy Ghost. I was embarrassed. People were talking about me. People were laughing at me. It was a hard, hard time for me. But I later discovered that losing those friends was a good thing. I learned that by trying to control me, they were not my friends to begin with.

> GOD IS SO GOOD THAT HE EVEN WORKS WHAT THE DEVIL MEANT FOR HARM FOR GOOD.

At first I didn't even understand what a real friend was. Secondly, losing all my friends drove me into a deep, personal and intimate relationship with Jesus because when He's all you've got, you can get real close to Him. Isaiah 30:18 says God is waiting to be good to you: *. . . therefore He lifts Himself up, that He may have mercy on you and show loving-kindness to you. For the Lord is a God of justice. Blessed (happy, fortunate, to be envied) are all those who [earnestly] wait for Him, who expect and look and long for Him [for His victory, His favor, His love, His peace, His joy, and His matchless, unbroken companionship]!*

This Scripture says that God is waiting to be good to somebody who is waiting for God to be good to them. What are you looking for in your life? What are you waiting for? What are you expecting? Are you expecting nothing? Are you expecting trouble, bad news or just "whatever"? That's a popular phrase today. "Whatever." My granddaughter says it. I'll say to her, "Do you want Grandma to buy you a new dress?"

"Whatever."

"Well, would you like to watch this movie?"

"Whatever."

"Do you want to go out to eat with me?"

"Whatever."

I'm thinking, **Stop with the whatever. Tell me what you want.** We've got to be careful about adopting that kind of attitude. "Whatever, you know. Who cares, whatever."

I'm not doing that. I've got specific things in my life, and I'm expecting favor, grace, mercy and goodness. I'm expecting my ministry to grow. I'm expecting to be on every television station in this world that's decent to be on.

I've prayed some bold prayers. I've asked God to let me help every human being on the face of the earth. I've said, "However many people one human being can help, I want to help that many." I don't want to just do a little bit of anything. I want to do everything that I can do and be all that I can be. We serve a good God.

God wants us then to let His character — which is good — to be developed in us. God wants us to display the fruit of goodness in our lives by being good to other people. God has never asked me to do anything that He doesn't show me first. He never asks me to be merciful to anybody else without giving me mercy. God would never ask us to forgive people who hurt us if He was not willing to forgive us first.

God is not asking any one of us to do anything that He has not already manifested in our own lives. He has deposited a seed in us of everything that He wants us to do. God is not going to ask me to love someone until He loves me first. That's why the love of God is shed abroad in my heart by the Holy Ghost. God says, "I love you free of charge. I give you grace, favor and mercy. I want to be kind and good to you." He's saying, "I'm patient with you."

Perhaps it would help if we would do some serious thinking about what God does for us: His longsuffering, kindness and mercy that is new every morning — His graciousness and generosity in our lives. Why do we need to be good to people? Because the Bible says in Romans 2:4 that it's the goodness of God that leads men to repentance. You can win somebody over quicker being good to them than anything imaginable. My brother was gone fourteen years, and during that time he never called. I thought we were close. I named my first child after him. He just disappeared, and I never heard from him for fourteen years. But when he came home, I didn't care about anything he had done. I didn't care about anything except . . . David's home. Everyone in my family cried.

I bought him a car and clothes. I took him out to eat. I love him. He's never done anything or been anywhere and I want to be good to him. It's in me because I know how good God has been to me. God has been so good to me. Why would I want to be legalistic by saying things like, "Well, you didn't call me, and you didn't care about me. And I'm not going to do anything for you because you don't deserve it."

Within two weeks of living in our house, David wanted Jesus. My brother said, "I don't know what it is you guys have got, but one thing is for sure, the world ain't got it. Whatever it is, I want it." He said, "I don't know whether you know it or not, but you guys are real strange. Do you have any idea how strange you are? All this love and goodness and . . . ."

The goodness of God leads men to repentance. We would not have to be beating everybody over the head with our Bible, begging them to take our Gospel tracts, pleading with them to let us tell them about Jesus if we'd just get out in the world and be good to people. They can't understand that.

Most of us may be willing to be good to a few folks when everything is going good for us. But one of the quickest ways out of your trouble has a twofold answer. Trust God and at the same time you're trusting God, be good to somebody. Trust God and do good. Trust God and do good. Trust God and do good. In Galatians 6:9 it says, *And let us not lose heart and grow weary and faint in acting nobly and doing right, for in due time and at the appointed season we shall reap, if we do not . . . faint.*

If God is telling people not to get discouraged, there must have been those who were going through trials. There must have been those who were having hard times. There must have been those who had been waiting for their breakthrough a long time because He said, "In due season, you will reap if you faint not." Keep doing what's right. Keep hanging in there. Don't be discouraged. God's going to come through for you. Verse 10 is in connection with what He's already said. He's already been talking about sowing and reaping and all these things, and then in verse 10 He says, *So then, as occasion and opportunity open up to us, let us do good to all people. . . .*

Each time you have an opportunity, be good to somebody. Don't let one occasion pass you by to be good to somebody that you don't jump in there and take advantage of that opportunity. If you want to be good to somebody, all you've got to do is listen to them. It doesn't take very long and they'll tell you something they want, something they need, something that's a problem for them. Then you can slip right in there and meet that need; just be a blessing, be good to them. The Bible says it's more blessed to give than to receive.

> EACH TIME YOU HAVE AN OPPORTUNITY, BE GOOD TO SOMEBODY.

You know what happens when somebody gives you a gift—you just get the gift. But when you give to somebody else, you get the **joy** of giving the gift. As occasion and opportunity open up, let us do good to all people, not only being useful or profitable to them, but also doing what is for their spiritual good and advantage. Be mindful to be a blessing. What does it mean to be mindful? It means to have your mind full of ways that you can be a blessing — and do it on purpose. Be mindful to be a blessing, especially to those of the household of faith — those who belong to God's family with you, the believer.

God says to start with the household of faith, start being good to brothers and sisters in Christ who need to be encouraged, who need to be edified and lifted up and exhorted. There are many ways we can be good to people. You can be good to somebody by giving them a word in due season. You can be good to somebody by praying for them. You can be good to somebody by telling them, "You look nice today." You can be good to somebody by giving them a gift. You can be good to somebody by baby-sitting for them.

There are many ways that we can be good to people. It doesn't always take money to be good to somebody. We need to be creative with ways to be good to people. There are so many selfish Christians. A woman told me yesterday that she's in a business where she deals with the public. She has customers that come in on a regular basis. She told me, "I used to love my business, but anymore I can hardly stand this business. It's not the business that changed; it's people who have changed."

She went on to say, "I have some of the same customers that I've had for years, but people are changing." She said, "People have no regard at all for you or how you feel or what you need." The whole push in the world today is self . . . "What about me?"

We as Christians must aggressively stand against that. I've had a total lifestyle change, even as a Christian, in the last ten or twelve years. I've been filled with the Holy Spirit and pursuing my ministry since 1976.

But even baptized in the Holy Spirit, even in full-time ministry, even with a growing ministry, I was not happy or content or satisfied. I discovered that I was never going to be happy if I got up every day and all I had on my mind was myself, my ministry, my need, my pain, my this, my that. God says, . . . *Be mindful to be a blessing, especially to those of the household of faith. . . .*[15]

The Bible tells us in 1 Peter 4:8 to let our love be heated up. First John 3:17 refers to closing your heart of compassion. God has given us a heart of compassion, but we can close it or we can open it. We have to do some things. We can't wait to feel like being good to somebody. We have to be intent on being good to somebody. Being good to others is spiritual warfare against Satan. We must be good in obedience to God and for our own personal joy and breakthrough.

The strongholds will come down if we start operating in the fruit of the Spirit.

I believe I carry a strong anointing on my life. I also believe there's a strong anointing on my preaching. That is not said out of pride. If I don't believe it's anointed, then I should sit down and shut up. I believe in my anointing, and I believe it's growing stronger every day. But there's a certain way that I must live my life behind the scenes. I'm not going to carry a strong anointing mistreating people when no one is looking.

We must be good to one another and get our minds off of ourselves. Scripture says that the rich are charged not to trust in uncertain riches but in the living God and they are charged to remember to do good to others and to be rich in good works.[16] He's saying to the rich people, "First of all, don't trust in your money. Don't put your hope in your riches. Keep your hope in the living God. Here's what you should do with your money. Be good to somebody."

He says to do good works. God gives us money and things so we can use the money and things to be a blessing to people. However, people take the money and the things and use people and money to bless themselves. That's an instruction for people that are rich. He says, "Here's what I want you to do. Walk in the fruit of the Spirit and be good to somebody; walk in love, be kind, be gentle, be merciful, be forgiving. Don't get in strife, don't have bitterness and resentment in your life." Hebrews 13:16 says, *Do not forget or neglect to do kindness and good, to be generous and distribute and contribute to the needy [of the church as embodiment and proof of fellowship], for such sacrifices are pleasing to God.* That Scripture tells me that if I'm going to be good to somebody, it's going to require sacrifice. I'm going to have to give up time and money and make an effort to do something that I would rather not do in the natural. It's by doing good that we allow the fruit of God's goodness to flow to us and **through** us.

CHAPTER 10

PATIENCE — LACKING NOTHING

Any time we become frustrated and get off into any kind of works, it is a sign that we are not being patient with God. By that I mean (unlike the psalmist in Psalm 40:1 who said, *I waited patiently and expectantly for the Lord; and He inclined to me and heard my cry*) we are not willing to wait on God and let Him do what He wants to do, in His way and time.

Patience is not waiting; it is how we act while we are waiting.

The hardest thing most of us ever have to do as Christians is wait on the Lord. But it is during the waiting periods of our life that the most powerful things are happening on the inside of us.

One definition of "patience" is long-suffering with mildness, gentleness and moderation. The best definition of "patience" I have ever heard is this: to be constant or to be the same all the time, no matter what is going on. That is my goal as a believer.

Patience is not an ability to wait. Patience is a fruit of the Spirit that manifests while we are waiting. If patience doesn't manifest in times of waiting, then we see the fruit of impatience during those times.

I used to be so impatient. Then one day God said to me in my heart, "Joyce, you might as well get over being impatient because you are going to spend most of your life waiting on something."

The bottom line is, everyone is going to wait. Waiting is not an option. And we do a lot more waiting in life than we ever do receiving so we may as well enjoy ourselves while God works out our problems.

WORKS VERSUS PATIENCE

I discovered a long time ago that when I became frustrated and fretful it was because I was trying to make something happen that only God could make happen.

Works are our energy trying to do God's job.

For example, if we are praying and believing for a breakthrough, sometimes it seems as if we wait and we believe and we pray, but nothing is happening. If we really want to know how we are to act in regard to patience during those times, all we need to do is look at the parable Jesus told about a farmer.[1]

The farmer sows his seed in the ground and then goes on his way, sleeping and rising. Eventually, the ground brings forth its yield on its own, without the man ever knowing when or how it is going to do so. The farmer doesn't know how the harvest will come or exactly when it will come, but his job is to get up in the morning, do his work and go to bed at night. He keeps up his patient vigil over the seed he's sown until he receives the harvest.

Jesus was telling us that is the way we should respond toward God. Our problem is that we are too impatient. We are continually asking God, "How are You going to do this? When are You going to do that?"

A farmer never knows how and when his crop is going to come in. He just keeps sleeping and rising, doing what he can to enrich his soil and cultivate his crops, but leaving the rest in the hands of the Creator.

ENJOY THE JOURNEY

We need to learn to do what we can do and not get frustrated trying to do things in our own strength and making things happen that only God can make happen. In other words, we need to learn how to enjoy the journey.

If you are waiting for your mate to come along, instead of becoming frustrated and upset, why not enjoy the time while you are single? You may say, "Well, I've been enjoying myself a long time."

Can I tell you something? If it's going to be next week, it will be next week. If it's going to be another five years, it's going to be another five years. There really is nothing you can do about it to make it happen sooner. So trust God and **prove** that you trust God. How do you do that? You prove that by enjoying the right-now life that He has given you.

We are not proving that we trust God if we go around depressed, sad, discouraged, negative, grumbling, murmuring and complaining all the time while we're waiting to receive the thing that we've asked God to give us. We are not showing that we can indeed be happy with Him and Him alone.

I had to become happy with a small ministry before God gave me a big one. I went through many things while I waited for my ministry to grow because sometimes I became frustrated and impatient. I like big. I like big jewelry. I like flashy clothes. I like a big car. I'm just that kind of person. If I'm going to do something, I want to make a statement. So I have a big car. When I come in, you're going to see me come in. I'm not doing it to impress people; that's just what I'm like. That's just the way I am.

So, of course, I wanted a big, big, big ministry. But it kept staying little, little, little, which really bothered me to the point that it stole my joy and my peace. The reason is that I did everything imaginable trying to make my ministry grow. I fasted and prayed and rebuked devils and pleaded and got people to agree with me in prayer. But my ministry stayed little because God had to teach me to be happy with Him and that if I never had a big ministry, I'd still love Him and serve Him.

One time when I was praying about my ministry God said to me in my spirit, "Joyce, if I asked you to go down by the riverfront and minister to fifty poor people the rest of your life, would you do it just because you love Me?"

Thank God, I had come to the point where I could sincerely say, "Yes, Lord, if I really know that's what You want me to do, then I can do that. I'll do that because I love You that much."

When we reach the point where we don't need to have things done our way and in our timing, that's when God will give them to us. So stay stable while you're making the journey and enjoy where you are at on the way to where you are going.[2]

Remember, patience is not waiting. It is how we act while we're waiting.

POSSESS YOUR SOUL

I love the Scripture in Luke 21:19 (KJV) that says, *In your patience possess ye your souls.* Your soul is your mind, your will and your emotions. It is that personality part of you — your thought life and your feelings.

If you don't learn to possess your own soul, or to control that
soulish life through developing the fruit of the
Spirit, then it will possess and control you.

> PATIENCE IS HOW
> WE ACT WHILE
> WE'RE WAITING.

So many people let their emotions rule
their lives.

How many times do we allow our day to be
ruined because someone hurts our feelings, and we become
offended? So for the rest of the day we go around feeling bad. There
is freedom and deliverance when we can say, "I'm not going to be
ruled by that hurt. I feel hurt, but I'm refusing to bow down to it."

That was a breakthrough for me when I stopped being ruled by
my emotions.

We are told in the Bible that we serve a God Who tests and tries
our emotions.[3] What does that mean? One thing it means is that He
will run you through things that will make you wait. Of course, God
could give you your breakthrough right now. I used to think, **Lord, I
know that You could do this. What is going on? Don't You love
me? Am I not doing something right? Don't I have enough faith?
Am I not praying enough? What is going on?**

We always think if we could find something else to **do**, then
God would give us our breakthrough. There are certain things we
need to do: read and meditate on the Word every day, spend time
alone with God on a regular basis, pray and fast and pray when God
tells us to. We need to give to others of ourselves, such as our time,
our money, a smile. Those are all part of our relationship with God,
and we need to do those things.

But more than anything, we need to develop this fruit of the
Spirit called patience in our life and just say, "Lord, I'm going to
trust You. If it takes longer than I'd like, then You must know
something that I don't know."

TRIALS DEVELOP PATIENCE

I've heard patience defined as a fruit of the Spirit that can only be developed under trial. Really, you cannot develop patience any other way. That means that the only way we ever develop the fruit of patience is by being around obnoxious people who drive us crazy; by waiting in traffic, waiting in grocery store lines, waiting for breakthroughs, waiting for our healing, waiting for people to change in our lives and waiting for ourselves to change.

Be patient with yourself; be patient with your own spiritual growth. Be patient with God if He's not coming through at the time that you'd like Him to. Be patient with people; be patient with circumstances; be patient because in patience you possess your soul. And James 1:4 says that the patient man is perfect and entire, *lacking in nothing.*

RECONCILE YOURSELF WITH THE WAYS OF GOD

You become patient when you reconcile yourself to the ways of God, when you know that you are in God's plan and His timing and that due time is God's time, that the appointed time is God's time. The bottom line is, God is not caught up in our time capsule and He is not in a hurry. He knows when we need what, and He will give it to us at the right time. Habakkuk 2:2,3 says to write your vision down; write it plainly; keep it in front of you, and don't be concerned if it's not happening yet because God will not be late, not one single day.

Why is God many times the God of the midnight hour? Why does He wait until the very last second to give you your breakthrough when He could have given you the exact same thing two months earlier and saved you all that pain? Is it because He is mean? Is it because He likes to watch us squirm? No, He is stretching our faith because when you get stretched, it gives you a greater capacity for that thing.

I want you to get a revelation of this because it will save you years of agony. I've been through all this. I was on this roller coaster, all the time, all my life. I tried to change Dave. I tried to change my kids. I tried to change myself. I tried to change my circumstances. I tried to make my ministry grow. I tried until I almost died. I was not enjoying my salvation. I was saved, and yes, maybe I was a little bit happier than somebody who wasn't saved. But you can't be happy without patience because if you don't have the fruit of patience, every time you turn around something is not going to happen when you want it to, the way you want it to. Somebody's not going to act the way you want them to and you're going to lose your joy and lose your peace and be all upset. Then you're going to act bad, and then you're going to be under condemnation.

You may say, "Well, then what can I do?"

Die. I'm not talking about physically dying; I'm talking about dying to self. Die to the way you want it. Die to the way you think it's got to be. Get it through your head that not everybody out there gets their own way, and if you don't get it your way, you're going to survive and live.

I used to just hate the fact that Dave got to watch the sports all the time. I didn't like sports. I didn't want him liking them, and he doesn't like one or two; he likes them all. When he'd watch them on TV, I used to lose my joy, and I'd pout and throw fits and carry on, and I would try to change that and change him, but it didn't change. The way you can get some patience, some peace and some joy in your life is to realize that not everything changes. There are some things that won't change.

LET GO AND LET GOD

One of the most frustrating things you can do is spend your life trying to do something about something you can't do anything about. I used to be an expert at that. I was trying to change me and change you and change this and change that. Finally, I just came into reconciliation with some things, and I started getting happy: "Lord, if You ever want to change it, You will change it; and if You don't, I'm staying happy anyway."

If you become desperate enough for some joy and peace, you'll start developing patience.

For instance, you sit in traffic; you've got cars in front of you, behind you and on both sides, so what is the sense of having a fit because you're going to arrive late anyway? Instead, look to the right, look to the left, look in front and behind and just say, "Well, praise the Lord."

God moves **two** different ways — **quickly and suddenly; slowly and little by little.** First, He always moves slowly, little by little, so slowly that you think it is never going to happen, and it's all you can do every day of your life to not give up.

Then **suddenly** God moves, and your breakthrough comes. You don't know how; you don't understand it, but it's just like, "That must have been God," because you've done everything that anybody could do forty-five times over and none of it worked. Finally, when you're done, God says, "Okay, now that you've finally finished, I'll take care of it."[4]

WAITING DESTROYS PRIDE

Deuteronomy 7:22 says that God delivers us from our enemies little by little lest the beasts of the field multiply among us. I believe that beast is pride. I think if God gave us everything the minute we wanted it, we would be so proud and haughty, we'd think it was us.

For example, if I pray and God gives me what I want right away, sometimes I begin to think, **Boy, my prayers are powerful. I must really be living a holy life. I'm a righteous person.**

That is a very wrong attitude to have. God's goodness is not based on our goodness. I have learned over the years that God's goodness in my life should only provoke praise and thanksgiving, not proud thoughts of how good I think I am.

God makes us wait because He is testing us. He told the Israelites, "I led you these forty years in the wilderness to test you and to prove you to see if you would keep My commandments or not."[5]

> GOD'S GOODNESS IS NOT BASED ON OUR GOODNESS.

It's one thing to keep the commandments of God when we're getting everything we want. It's another thing to keep the commandments of God when we're not getting much of what we want. It's one thing to be nice to somebody when they're being nice to you. It's another thing entirely to operate in the fruit of the Spirit when they're not being so nice to you.

GOD'S WAYS, GOD'S TIME

Proverbs 16:2 says, *All the ways of a man are pure in his own eyes, but the Lord weighs the spirits (the thoughts and the intents of the heart).* Then verse 9 says, *A man's mind plans his way, but the Lord directs his steps and makes them sure.* I like that because my mind can be planning my way, but then God directs my path in another direction that I may not understand because it's not my plan.

Thank God that, even though your mind plans it one way, He is able to lead your steps in a totally different direction — sometimes all we know to plan is what we have reference to right then. That's all we know because we don't know anything else. But God does a whole lot of things that we don't know.

Then in verse 25, we're told, *There is a way that seems right to a man and appears straight before him, but at the end of it is the way of death.* God's ways may not always be quick and speedy, but there is an appointed time. In other words, God has an appointment with your circumstance. God has an appointment with your breakthrough. God has got an appointment with your answered prayer.

Suppose you make an appointment at the doctor for 11:45 on a certain day. You've had that appointment for a long time, and you've been waiting for that appointment. Now, if you showed up there for your appointment at 9:00 A.M., it wouldn't matter how frustrated you got or how much you paced around the office or what kind of fit you threw. You would still have to wait for your appointment until your appointment time.

As we have seen, the Bible says that God has an appointed time. We also see this in Acts 1:6,7 when some of the disciples said to Jesus, *Lord, is this the time when You will reestablish the kingdom and restore it to Israel?* In other words, they were saying, "Jesus, tell us when You're going to come back. We want to know when these things are going to happen. Tell us the **time** that it's going to take place. What is the **time** these things are going to happen?"

Jesus said to them, "It is not for you to know the appointed time. Only God knows the appointed time."

So if only God knows the appointed time, (and I believe that God is so awesome and great and so smart and so wonderful and so good) and if I believe He loves me, then why can't I believe that at the appointed time I'm going to get my breakthrough? Why can't I just prove that I believe that by going ahead and enjoying my life and being peaceful and patient while I'm waiting?

Do you agree that you cannot be happy if you don't have patience? Do you agree that if you don't have patience you're not going to treat people right?

PUT ON PATIENCE

In Colossians 3:12 (NASB) we are told to *put on* patience. That tells me that patience is something that I have to do on purpose. Just because I don't feel patient doesn't mean I don't have to act patiently. That's what *put on* means.

The Amplified Bible version of that Scripture says, *Clothe yourselves therefore, as God's own chosen ones. . . .* Let me ask you a question. When you get up in the morning and put your clothes on, have you ever just stood in your closet and had your clothes jump off the rack and get on your body? Have your clothes ever just jumped off the hanger and got on your body and you just didn't have to do anything — you just stood there? Or have you ever just stood there and said, "I want clothes. I pray for clothes; clothes, get on my body"?

In the same way, we have to *put on* patience. We can pray for patience, but the Bible says that's not enough.

PREPARE MENTALLY

One of the things that I've really been studying lately is 1 Peter 1:13 which says we are to gird up the loins of our mind. What does that mean? It means to prepare mentally for something.

We need to have a mental preparation for things. If we don't have any kind of a mental preparation, and we think that everything is just going to go our way every day, then when things don't go our way, we will act badly and fall apart.

Colossians 3 says, *Set your mind and keep it set.* The best time to do that is to set our minds in the morning. Before we get out of bed say, "OK, Lord, I want to operate in the fruit of the Spirit today. And I've been around the block a few times, God. I already know that probably everything is not going to go my way today. I know that probably there's going to be some things that are going to happen that I didn't plan for; some things are going to happen that I will wish did not happen that way. The phone's going to ring when I don't want it to. Somebody's going to knock on the door when I don't want them to. Somebody's going to ask me to do something I don't want to do, and yet it's somebody that I feel like I need to do it for.

"I'm going to get a phone call that is going to interrupt my whole day. And all of a sudden, I'm going to have to go in this direction when I wanted to go in that direction. Somebody's going to have a problem that I have to deal with. I'm going to walk in my office, and someone is going to tell me something that I'm going to have to deal with that I don't want to deal with. Lord, I am going to set my mind to be patient today no matter what happens."

I used to get so aggravated. I'd walk in my office and someone would say, "There's a problem," and I would say, "I don't want to deal with that today."

Then I would say to Dave, "When will we ever get to the point where we don't have to deal with something all the time?" and Dave would say, "Never."

I didn't like that, but Dave doesn't stay upset all the time because he already knows that there will always be something to deal with. He would tell me, "Joyce, cast your care, and decide not to be upset."

Set your mind. Gird up the loins of your mind. Tell yourself, "Whatever happens today, I can be patient because I have the fruit of patience in me."

If you set your mind, you're going to have a lot of victories. If you don't set your mind, Satan is going to catch you off guard, and if you're not ready for something mentally, then you're not ready for it.

We have this kind of thinking that "If I don't get my breakthrough next week, I can't stand it. I've got to have my breakthrough next week or I can't stand it. If you do this one more time, I can't stand it. If this happens one more time, I'm going to fall apart."

What are you doing? Every single time you think like that or talk like that, you're setting yourself up for a disaster. You may even think that when you do that you're threatening God.

YOU CAN TAKE IT

I remember sitting out on my patio one day many years ago, and I'd just had it so I said, "That's it, God, I want to tell You right now that I cannot take any more of this. You've got to do something, God, right now. **I cannot take any more of this!**"

He said to me in my spirit, "Yes, you can."

That surprised me and I said to Him, "What makes You think that I can?"

He said, "I know you can because my Word says that I will never put more on you than what you can bear, but with every temptation I will also provide the way out.⁶ And if this is what you have to deal with right now, then you've got to trust Me. You can stand it because I am going to hold you up and help you to stand it. So quit saying you can't stand it because things that you've told Me before you couldn't stand, you stood and here you still are, alive."

Remember, we are to put on patience. As Colossians 3:12 says, we are to clothe ourselves as God's own chosen ones, . . . *(His own picked representatives), [who are] purified and holy and well-beloved [by God Himself, by putting on behavior marked by] . . . patience. . . .* It was such a revelation to me when I realized that I could put on behavior.

Really, that is a decision. It's not about how godly you are or how full of the Holy Spirit you are. There will be times when you want to knock somebody's head off. But the difference in somebody who feels like doing it but who doesn't do it is that they've developed the fruit of the Spirit in their lives, and they've chosen to live by that fruit to honor God. It is not because they feel like it, or don't feel like it.

When you see that kind of stable person, it's not because they never feel anything. It's because they've learned to possess their soul and not let their soul possess them. They've learned that when they feel something and God says, "No, that's not the way I want it to be," then they reach out there and they get all those feelings and they just bring them in line with the Word of God.

RIGHT BEHAVIOR IS A DECISION

When you choose to live that way, there will be times when you hurt so bad you may feel like your insides are going to fall out on the floor. I've had times when I've had to run into my bathroom and shove a towel in my mouth to keep from talking back to my husband.

Just like your clothes don't jump on you, the right kind of behavior is not going to jump on you. You have to decide "I can be nice to you. I'm going to love you. I'm going to keep on giving you presents. Even if you never say thank you. I'm going to keep on blessing you even if you never bless me back. I'm going to keep on praying for you. You're not stealing my joy. You're not stealing my peace. I'm going to keep on keeping on until I wear the devil out."

When you're having personal problems in your life, the last thing you want to do is back off your ministry. That's the time to keep on doing everything exactly the same as you would do it if you didn't have one single solitary problem. What happens to you while that's happening? You're growing and maturing spiritually.

If you have asked God for something that He has in mind for you, He's in agreement with you. He wants to give it to you, and He's got it all prepared. But I've learned that God has to prepare you before you can receive the thing that He has prepared for you.

Every time we ask God to bring us up to another level, a little bit more of our flesh has got to go by the wayside. That doesn't mean that all of our problems came from God. But it means that God is going to use our problems to prepare us for the beautiful things He has planned for us.

I believe that when we go through problems, God thinks, "I'm just going to get good use out of this. The devil means this for your harm, but I'm going to work it out for your good. While I'm solving the problem, you might as well get some benefit out of this. You might as well get some more patience. You might as well get some more fruit. You might as well get some more trust. Your faith might as well grow."

Oh, it took me so many years to learn that, but once I did, it was so wonderful to be free!

It is not freedom if you have to stay mad three days every time somebody hurts your feelings or doesn't do what you want them to do. That is not freedom. That is bondage to the max. It is not freedom when you are so full of pride that you cannot say, "I'm sorry." It is not freedom when you can never let anybody else think they're right even if you know they're not. Why do we work so hard to prove that we're right? We do that because we really don't know who we are in Christ.[7] We don't feel right about ourselves so we have to be right about everything to feel right.

LOVE IS PATIENT

Colossians 3:12 continues, *putting on . . . patience . . . [which is tireless and longsuffering, and has the power to endure whatever comes, with good temper.* One of the greatest ways that we can show love to other people is by being patient with them. That doesn't mean we don't deal with issues or become a doormat for everyone to walk all over us all the time.

There are times when we have to deal with circumstances. But I'm the kind of person who deals with everything, and it doesn't take me very long to do it. I had to learn that a lot of times God didn't want me to deal with something right away because I may have been ready, but the other person wasn't ready. And if I don't move in God's timing and let God get them ready, then I can destroy somebody with my quick, straight-to-the-point approach.

My brother, Dave, is a good example of that. He was a new believer, and when he used to live in my house, I saw lots of things that I wanted to change in him. For instance, when he'd get up in the morning at five o'clock and go turn the television on, I wanted to go say to him, "Dave, why don't you pray and read the Bible? That television is not really good for you at five o'clock in the morning."

Or, if I'd wake up at two o'clock in the morning and hear him downstairs with the TV on, I wanted to get my robe on and go downstairs and say, "You need to turn that thing off."

The time came when God had me do that, but God made me wait several weeks because you can't just dump everything on a person at once. If things are not done in God's timing, then we hurt people. We destroy them and it's too much for them to handle.

God prepared my brother's heart. By the time I went and talked to him, in his heart he already was starting to know he shouldn't watch so much television.

When we begin to recognize a wrong behavior in someone, it is often God trying to lead us to pray for them. If we pray first, that opens the door for God to deal with them. Then He can prepare their heart for any future action He might ask us to take.

We try so hard to make things happen, and we get so impatient and so frustrated we don't realize that if we pray, God has a plan. His plan may not always be our plan, but we've got to get sensitive and listen to God about what He wants us to deal with and what He doesn't.

So when I say be patient, I don't mean never deal with anything; I mean to be patient enough to deal with things in God's timing and not our own timing.

PRAYER INSTEAD OF IMPATIENCE

One of the greatest ways to show love to others is to be patient with them — patient with their weaknesses and faults, patient with their slowness — like with slow clerks, new clerks or sometimes even no clerks when you're in a store.

I finally got patient with the slow clerks, and now I've started getting no clerks. I finally realized that it is a test.

If you don't pass this time, you'll get to take it over. I mean, you'll get clerks in training, clerks who run out of change, clerks who have to replace the tape in the register and don't know how to, clerks who are rude, clerks who talk on the phone the entire time they're waiting on you, or they ignore you and don't wait on you at all because they're on a personal phone call, clerks who leave the metal detectors on your purchase causing you to either get embarrassed because people think you're a thief when you leave the store or if you do get out of the store, you must return to the store the next day because if you try to take the thing off, it's got some kind of liquid in it that will ruin your clothes. One time I had that happen to me twice in one week from the same store.

What good does it do to get impatient? It's not going to change anything. So often we get impatient when what we should do is pray.

BE PATIENT

Let's look at some other areas where we need to be patient:

Be patient with people's different opinons.

Be patient with people's personalities. We all have people in our lives who have personalities that are harder for us to handle. That's an opportunity to exercise the fruit of patience.

Be patient when someone tells you a story for the third time, even though you mentioned in the beginning, "Yes, you told me that last week." You're trying to be nice, and you're trying to be loving, but you're thinking, **Oh, God, not again. This is a long story.**

Be patient when someone wants to tell you every minor detail of a story that you're not even interested in hearing.

Be patient when people interrupt you when you don't want to be interrupted. My husband likes to read to me sometimes whenever I'm studying. He will be reading something that is totally different from what I'm working on, and he will say, "Joyce, listen to this."

Now, when I'm writing or when I'm studying, I get really deep into it. And I don't even know what's going on around me. But Dave is my husband and I need to submit and show respect. Really, I know what he's feeling. When we are excited about something, we want somebody to be excited with us. So I can show him love by stopping what I'm doing and giving him my attention for a little bit because I get to share with people all the time. Sometimes people just need someone to listen to them because what they want to say is important to them. So one of the things that we can do for people is just listen to them a little bit.

- Be patient with people when they call you at 6:00 A.M. and say, "Oh, weren't you up yet? I've been up for an hour."

- Be patient when people goof around and act silly while you're trying to be serious.

- Be patient when you're sick and going through a really rough time and people seem to be clueless concerning your needs.

- Be patient when people push in front of you in line or take a parking space you've been waiting for somebody to pull out of.

- Be patient when a department store heavily advertises a certain item on sale, and when you get there, they're all on back order.

- Be patient with a clerk when you have to return an item two times because it fell apart both times you took it home.

- Be patient when you buy a pair of shoes and you get home with two different sizes in the same box.

IN ITS TIME

Ecclesiastes 3:11 tells us that God makes *everything beautiful in its time*. Notice that verse says **in** its time, **not** out of its time. By now you are probably thinking, **If I understand what you're saying, there is no telling how long I may need to wait sometimes.**

That's right.

But when you know that you are in God's hands, it doesn't matter to you how long you have to wait, and it will probably happen a lot sooner than you think.

If God does shorten the time, it will be because you have put yourself totally in His hands and said, "Lord, any time You decide is fine with me. I love You, and I'm going to just keep on enjoying myself until You bring forth what You know is best for me — in its time."

CHAPTER 11

KINDNESS — EASY TO GET ALONG WITH

Some of us are a little more naturally disposed toward kindness than others. Many of us find we can be kind to those who are kind to us, but I think we all run into trouble when we try to be kind to those we don't think deserve kindness. The truth is kindness should be extended to people because they don't deserve it; otherwise, it's not kindness.

If you look up the word *mercy*, you'll find that part of the definition of mercy is to be kind.[1] Likewise, if you look up the word *kindness*, you'll find that part of the definition is to be merciful.[2] Kindness gives blessings to those that don't deserve it, and God will put it on your heart to bless people who have hurt you.

Has God ever asked you to do something really special for somebody who hurt you? When God does that, we think it will turn us inside out. There is nothing in our "want-to" that desires to do that, but doing it anyway is "power living."

When we choose to operate in certain kingdom principles, they bring us into a place in life I call "power living." The Bible says some of the ways we can live powerful lives are to bless our enemies, pray for those who hurt us and despitefully use us, and be kind to them.[3] The Bible also promises us in Luke 6:35 that we will receive a reward from God **after** we have been kind to other people.

As a kind person, the devil might try to convince you that you're always the one that's giving and you never receive anything. You

GOD REWARDS US FOR BEING KIND TO PEOPLE.

might spend a lot of time in your life blessing someone who never blesses you, but God Himself will bless you — He might use someone else to bless you.

Kindness withholds due punishment. God is so patient and longsuffering because He is kind. All the fruits work together. Kindness requires self-control.

Matthew 11:28 says, *Come to Me, all you who labor and are heavy-laden and overburdened, and I will cause you to rest. [I will ease and relieve and refresh your souls.]* That is a wonderful invitation. It speaks volumes to me.

Jesus said, *Come to Me . . . .* He didn't say, "If you deserve it, I will give it to you." He just said to come because *God is love,*[4] and love always gives. Love is always giving something that other people can benefit from.

I've found a giver has to have a recipient. In the last several years, God has done a big work in that area of my life. It's something that we grow into gradually — I believe I have grown into a giver.

There's a difference between one who gives and a giver. Giving is a lifestyle for a giver. A giver looks for ways to give to and bless people because it becomes part of what you do to be happy within yourself. If I want to be happy, I must be a giver.

It bothers me if I'm trying to give something to someone and they won't take it. It's much easier for me if they'll just take it and say thank you. I'm not trying to draw attention, but I have to give to be happy.

It's God's nature to give. He has to give, and you'd be amazed at how many people refuse to receive God's mercy because they think they don't deserve it; and they're right, they don't deserve mercy. If you ever deserve mercy, then it's no longer mercy.

We really don't desire all that mercy, grace and favor are. God is doing outrageous, wonderful things for people who don't deserve it.

God has given my brother awesome breakthroughs. It seems every time he turns around someone blesses him, and he doesn't deserve that. God put it in our hearts to bring him into our home. We bought him a car, clothes and a ring for Christmas. He is like the prodigal son. He has a ring on his finger, shoes on his feet and a robe on his back.

He was gone fourteen years and never picked up the telephone one time to call me. He didn't say, "Happy Birthday, Sis. How are you?" But I understand. It really blessed me when I saw my reaction to him when he came home. I knew by how I responded that God had indeed changed me greatly. Before God worked in my life through His Word and Spirit, I would have been bitter, resentful, judgmental, revengeful — but none of those wrong responses even occurred to me when Dave came home.

When we received his phone call and he said he was coming home, I could not wait for him to show up at the airport. I didn't think about any of those years. They were instantly forgotten because now he was home and that was the thing that mattered to me now.

I wanted to bless him and make his life good. I desired for him to see the goodness of God. I knew when he experienced the goodness of God, he would never want to serve anyone other than God.

That's why God pours His kindness upon us when we don't deserve it. He wants us to know how good He is. It's the goodness of God that leads men to repentance.[5] We need to be good to people. How could we ever hope our witness has any power if we aren't kind and merciful to people?

Once you get over the hump and kindness becomes a lifestyle, you'll find it's really not hard anymore. It becomes fun because you see the reward. You realize what it can do to the devil. Every time you're good to somebody that doesn't deserve it, it defeats Satan. He hates that.

Several years ago, my daughter Sandra had lost a prescription of medicine that had just been filled for her. She apparently set it on the sink, knocked it into the trash can and we threw it away. That same day she made chocolate chip cookies and burned all of them. We had to go get more chocolate chips.

I was mad at her and said, "You are going to pay for that medicine and those chocolate chips. You're not paying attention to what you're doing. You're wasting money."

A few days later twelve dollars showed up on my dresser with a note that said, "This is for the chocolate chips and the medicine." It just so happened I was studying the fruit of kindness that day. I took her money back to her and said, "This is your blessing day. I'm teaching on the fruit of kindness tonight. Here's your money back."

How could I be rigid with her after studying Scriptures on kindness all day? God's Word changed my heart, and it eventually changed my life.

Sometimes we are like that when somebody hurts us. We always want them to pay. I found a liberating Scripture in Matthew 18.

Verses 23-27 tell about the man who owed the king money and when the king came to settle the accounts, the guy didn't have the money. The king let him off the hook and said, "I'll forgive you." The master said, "Pay me what you owe me," and *The Amplified Bible* says that the man *could not pay*.

I got such a revelation out of that. I spent many years in my life trying to collect from people that had hurt me that could not pay me back. If someone takes your virginity or your dignity through abuse, they can't give that back to you. They don't know how to give it back to you. That's why the Bible says, *Vengeance is Mine, I will repay (requite), says the Lord.*[6]

Payment comes in two ways. You can rest assured if your enemies aren't straightened out yet, then you know the vengeance of God is ultimately going to come. God not only says He will take care of your enemies, but He will take care of you. God will reward you and give you "double for your trouble."

If someone is not treating you right, He will repay you. Isaiah 61:7 says that for our former shame and our former abuses, God will give us a twofold reward or double honor. That only happens if we don't try to take care of it in ourselves.

We spend so much time in our life trying to take care of ourselves. The more we try to take care of ourselves, the more we limit what God can do for us. I'm limited and God is not. Even if God let everything I was trying to do for myself work out, I'd still be limited.

Bless and do good to your enemies seems like another upside down principle that doesn't make any sense to us, but the Bible promises your reward from God will be rich and intense. It is very possible that you have not been able to figure out why you're not being blessed. Part of the reason may be because you have not sown seeds of kindness in people's lives. The Bible says if we give mercy to others, then we'll receive mercy from God when we need mercy.[7] We reap what we sow.[8]

Matthew 11:29 and 30 say, *Take My yoke upon you and learn of Me, for I am gentle (meek) and humble (lowly) in heart, and you will find rest (relief and ease and refreshment and recreation and blessed quiet) for your souls. For My yoke is wholesome (useful, good — not harsh, hard, sharp, or pressing, but comfortable, gracious, and pleasant), and My burden is light and easy to be borne.*

We might say it like this: "All you that are tired, weary and worn out from trying to take care of things yourself and the world has run all over you, come to Me, and you'll find out that I'm good, kind and merciful. I won't be hard on you. I'll work with you. We'll take care of it. If you're tired of living that way, then just come to Me." It's a simple invitation.

When God throws a party, it's a come-as-you-are party. We don't have to get all fixed up. When my brother came home, he came as he was.

Look at Lamentations 3:19,20: *[O Lord] remember [earnestly] my affliction and my misery, my wandering and my outcast state, the wormwood and the gall. My soul has them continually in remembrance and is bowed down within me.*

There are several good lessons there. The writer tells us he has his mind on all his problems and his soul is bowed down within him with sorrow.

He says in verse 21, *But this I recall and therefore have I hope and expectation.* Now he makes a turn. He said, "OK, I'm going to get something else in my mind that gives me hope and the expectation of good." The thing that he begins to think about pulls him out of this pit. Then in verses 22-24 he says: *It is because of the Lord's mercy and loving-kindness that we are not consumed, because His [tender] compassions fail not. They are new every morning; great and abundant is*

Your stability and faithfulness. The Lord is my portion or share, says my living being (my inner self); therefore will I hope in Him and wait expectantly for Him.

However, the writer's positive thoughts brought him out of the depressed, miserable state he was in. When we think about our problems, we sink lower and lower, but thoughts about the goodness, mercy, kindness and faithfulness of God give us hope.

Verse 25 says, *The Lord is good to those who wait hopefully and expectantly for Him, to those who seek Him [inquire of and for Him and require Him by right of necessity and on the authority of God's word].*

The Bible says God is good to those who wait for Him and expect Him to be good to them. It isn't that we deserve it, but it is available to those who expect God to be good to them.

We look at our problems far too much instead of God's character. Mercy is part of His character; therefore, we don't have to talk God into mercy. All we need to do is receive it.

As a young woman, born again, filled with the Spirit and in ministry, I had no idea that I had such a problem with mercy. I had probably preached messages on mercy, but God kept giving me Matthew 9:13, that says, *Go and learn what this means: I desire mercy [that is, readiness to help those in trouble] and not sacrifice and sacrificial victims. For I came not to call and invite [to repentance] the righteous (those who are upright and in right standing with God), but sinners (the erring ones and all those not free from sin).* Jesus said, "I didn't come for the well; I came for the sick."[9]

> GOD'S GOODNESS IS AVAILABLE TO THOSE WHO EXPECT HIM TO BE GOOD TO THEM.

If we were all fixed up, we wouldn't have needed Jesus to start with. I needed God and wanted to stay desperate for Him. I continued to hear Him say, *Go and learn what this means: I desire mercy.*

It's a long story, but the summation of it is after God continued to give me that Scripture, I finally began to study mercy.

Remember, mercy is kindness. It took a long time for me to get what I'm telling you, but I found out two things. I was not a merciful person. I was very legalistic and rigid. I had a way I wanted things done and that's the way I wanted it done. I wasn't too willing to give an inch in either direction. If I didn't get it the way I wanted it, although the person did their best and really couldn't give me what I wanted, I became upset with them. I wasn't merciful. I refused to give them some liberty.

Long before that, I had reached a place where I wanted to be merciful with all my heart, but I wasn't able to be. I would become angry because I'd see other people be merciful, and I wanted that in my life.

I learned that I was not merciful to other people. Then God went a step further with me and showed me that when He says "Go and learn what mercy means," there are two sides to it. We have to learn how to receive the mercy of God before we can give the mercy of God.

I had a hard time being merciful because I wouldn't receive mercy. I was very legalistic with myself, and therefore, very legalistic with everyone else. The Bible says you are to love your neighbor as you love yourself. You had better look at how you treat yourself because sometimes you try to give something to someone that you don't have yourself.

If you don't receive the love of God and love yourself in a balanced way, how can that love flow through you to anybody else? If you don't receive the mercy of God when you make mistakes, you don't have a reservoir to give out from whenever you need to give mercy away.

I've become a very merciful person, and I enjoy the mercy of God every day. God has no trouble with me anymore. I receive mercy. When I sin, I receive mercy the next second. I'm sorry for the mistakes I make, but I refuse to live under condemnation. I've read too many times the Scripture in the Bible that says *There is therefore now no condemnation.*[10] Or the Scriptures that say to repent, ask God to forgive you, admit your sins, receive the mercy of God and go on. Mercy is for people who don't deserve it.

Colossians 3:12 says we should have behavior full of mercy. God mightily uses people who are meek, patient and kind. Sometimes we view these qualities as weaknesses. The world says you're wimpy if you're meek and patient.

The world wants to know, "Why are you letting them treat you like that?" If you're kind to people, they say, "Why are you doing that? Don't you know people are going to walk all over you if you treat them like that?" Fear of being taken advantage of chokes the fruit of kindness.

I'm going to act the way God tells me to act because the Bible says if I will do that, then God will reward me. When you are kind to people, you should aggressively believe God for a reward to come into your life because you're doing it out of your love for God.

There are many men and women in the Bible that God used, and we call them giants of faith, but they were people just like you and me. If you want to be a great man or woman of God, you have to be kind and merciful. Mercy goes to people who don't deserve it. Mercy blesses those who should be punished.

As I mentioned previously, in Genesis 37, Joseph's brothers mistreated him badly. They were jealous of him because his father loved him and gave him a special coat. Joseph had dreams and visions for his life. The Bible says they were so jealous they hated him.

It is amazing when everyone is not excited about your dreams and visions. Everyone is not excited about your blessings. Sometimes it's hard to find someone you can share your blessings with and believe they're going to be genuinely excited for you.

Joseph's brothers threw him in a pit and then sold him into slavery. They told their father he was dead. While in Egypt many circumstances and situations occurred that were unfair. He spent thirteen years in prison for something he didn't do. He had many opportunities for bitterness.

Do you ever have opportunity for bitterness? It will not do you one bit of good. You may feel like your whole life has been stolen by people who have mistreated you, and now, you're bitter! If you stay bitter, what they did to you will steal your future. Bitterness does not make you better than the person who hurt you; it actually brings you down to their level.

Joseph was promoted by God, and he had charge of all the food supply in Egypt. That is a good place to be when there is a famine in the land. The brothers had to go to Joseph, not even knowing that Joseph was their brother. When they saw him, they recognized him and fell down before him because they thought he was going to kill them or in some way repay them for the things they had done.

They knew that if Joseph mistreated them, they deserved it. In Genesis 50:18-21 *The Amplified Bible* says, *Then his brothers went and fell down before him, saying, See, we are your servants (your slaves)! And Joseph said to them, Fear not; for am I in the place of God? [Vengeance is His, not mine.] As for you, you thought evil against me, but God meant it for good, to bring about that many people should be kept alive, as they are this day. Now therefore, do not be afraid. I will provide for and support you and your little ones. And he comforted them [imparting cheer, hope, strength] and spoke to their hearts [kindly].*

What a man! It takes a real man of God to offer kindness and mercy to those who have mistreated you.

In Genesis 13, Abraham was kind to Lot, his nephew, who would have had nothing if it wouldn't have been for Abraham. Strife came between Abraham and Lot's herdsmen and workers. Abraham went to Lot and said, "Look, we need to separate because our herdsmen are in strife and this is not going to work. I pray you let there be no strife between us." Abraham was so nice and so kind. He said, "I'll tell you what. You pick whichever part of the valley that you want, and I'll take what's left over." Obviously, Lot took the best part of the valley. Abraham said, "That's fine. Be blessed."

Then God took Abraham up on a hill and He said, "OK, now look north, south, east and west, and however far you can see, Abraham, it's yours."

When people seem to use us, the devil screams in our ears, "Well, you're letting them take something away from you. They're stealing it. Don't you know that's not right; that's not fair. They wouldn't have had anything if it wouldn't have been for you." That's when you say, "No, they're not taking anything away from me. I'm giving it to them. I'll bless them and be good to them. God will take care of me. I'd rather have God take care of me than people take care of me, anyway."

In the eighth book of the Bible, Ruth, we find another example of kindness and the faithfulness of God. Ruth was kind to Naomi whose husband had died. Ruth's husband, one of Naomi's sons, had also died. Another daughter-in-law, Orpha, went back to her family after her husband died. But Ruth said, "I'm going to stay with you, Naomi." Naomi was an older woman and she needed somebody to be with her.

Ruth and Naomi went to the country where Naomi was from and when they got there, they had no food and no provision. Ruth went out into the field of Boaz and gleaned in the fields, which meant she went along behind the reapers and picked up whatever tiny bits of grain happened to be left from the day. They were trying to feed themselves on that.

In response to her kindness to Naomi, God spoke to Boaz, the owner of this field, who was the richest man in the county. God said to him, "I want you to leave handfuls for her on purpose."

If you are kind to people everywhere you go in your life, you're going to find handfuls God left on purpose, lying around for you. You will have a pile of blessings here and there. It's so exciting to serve God like this because you begin to see the things God can do for you that no other person would do. I told God a few years ago, "I want You to bless me so much that I just go around all the time with my mouth hanging open in awe."

MERCY PRECEDES HEALING

I believe that mercy must precede healing. Many times we try to deserve a healing. "I've prayed right; I've done this and that right; now heal me." But in Matthew 20:30-31, it says, *And behold, two blind men were sitting by the roadside, and when they heard that Jesus was passing by, they cried out, Lord, have pity and mercy on us. . . . The crowds reproved them and told them to keep still; but they cried out all the more, Lord, have pity and mercy on us. . . .* The Bible says Jesus stopped.

He was on His way somewhere and these guys cried out, "Jesus! Have mercy on us." He didn't know them. Jesus could have said, "I don't know you." The crowd was saying, "Shut up. Quit bothering Him. He doesn't want to mess with you." They just cried out all the more. "Jesus! Have mercy on us." Jesus stopped.

And in Matthew 20:32-34 *The Amplified Bible* says, *And Jesus stopped and called them, and asked, What do you want Me to do for you? They answered Him Lord, we want our eyes to be opened! And Jesus, in pity, touched their eyes; and instantly they received their sight.* . . . The cry of mercy stops Jesus.

We don't cry out for enough mercy. We spend too much time trying to deserve God's goodness. In Luke 17:12-19, lepers cried out for mercy, and they all received healing, but only one came back to give Him thanks. In Matthew 15:22-28, a woman from the Canaanite district said with a loud and urgent cry, *Have mercy on me, O Lord, Son of David! My daughter is miserably and distressingly and cruelly possessed by a demon!* Her daughter was delivered.

In Matthew 17:15 we see a man whose son had epilepsy, and he came and said, *Have mercy on my son, for he has epilepsy* . . . and *frequently he falls into the fire and many times into the water.* Jesus stopped again. Jesus left one town and was on his way to another town. It seems like every time He went a few blocks, somebody said, "Oh, Jesus! Have mercy on me." And He stopped and talked to them.

> WE SPEND TOO MUCH TIME TRYING TO DESERVE GOD'S GOODNESS INSTEAD OF SIMPLY RECEIVING IT.

What would happen in our lives if we stopped when we had a chance to be kind and merciful? If we would sow seeds of kindness and mercy, we would find handfuls on purpose all along our pathway.

I think about this when I'm shopping, walking through crowded parking lots and malls with all the rude people that will hurt you to get the last thing that's on sale. Dave and I call them mall demons. I refuse to fight with someone over a piece of merchandise that I probably don't even need anyway. I would rather humble myself and wait on God to get me what I need. As a result, I have found when we do go shopping, we often find sales we were not expecting. Yes, God will take care of us if we treat others the way He would treat them. Showing mercy instead of judgment brings a reward. It opens the door to exciting, exceptional living.

Psalm 23:6 KJV closes with, *Surely goodness and mercy shall follow me all the days of my life.* Goodness and mercy are following you around. You can't get away from them because they are everywhere. I decided to quit running from them and run into them.

My favorite story of running to mercy in the Bible is blind Bartimaeus in Mark 10:46,47. It says that blind Bartimaeus cried out, *Jesus, Son of David, have pity and mercy on me [now]!* In *The Amplified Bible, now* has a big exclamation mark. In other words, he didn't want to wait for his mercy. He wanted his mercy now!

BUT FOR THE GRACE OF GOD THERE GO I

Paul said an interesting thing. He said, "I received mercy from God because I had acted in ignorance."[11] Paul, who once was Saul, persecuted Christians. The Bible says he aggressively and vehemently persecuted Christians and gathered them up to be stoned, beaten and jailed.[12] He was really ignorant because he felt like he was doing God a service. Saul didn't understand the new covenant. When God appeared to him on the Damascus road, he received Christ. The scales fell from his eyes, and he saw truth. God called that man to be the one who brought the message of grace to the Church. Paul, more than anyone, could understand the grace of God because he knew what he was and he would say things like, "But for the grace of God, there go I."

If we can really understand how much mercy and grace it takes for God to love us, then we can love other people. I love that statement Paul said, *I received mercy from God because I acted in ignorance.* Jesus on the cross said, *Father, forgive them; for they know not what they do.*[13] Stephen, while being stoned, said, *Lord, fix not this sin upon them [lay it not to their charge]!*[14]

Why did Jesus and those godly men pray like that? They understood there are people who have been deceived, and don't know how to behave any better.

My daughter told me recently that her goal this year was to learn to love or to treat with kindness and goodness every single person that she ran into who was nasty to her. She said, "That's my goal. I want to submit to God in my emotions and the way that I handle myself so that when I'm out in the public and someone mistreats me, I respond in kindness."

She said, "One of the things that God has shown me that really helps me to do this, is when someone is grouchy with me, I can stand there and think, **I don't know what they're going through. Maybe right now their back hurts so badly they can hardly stand there at that cash register. Maybe they've got a horrible migraine headache. Maybe they have a child that just died. Maybe their husband walked off on them and is living with another woman. Maybe they've just been told they're losing their job this Friday.**"

We don't understand what's going on in people's lives.

Kindness will cause you to slow down and give people some time. People are under so much stress that half the time they don't even know what they're doing. Life was not meant to be the way it is today. We were not meant to live at the fast pace that we live at with thousands of things coming at us at once. If you go to a foreign country, the pace slows down unbelievably. Americans seem to be overloaded in every area. Stress is the disease of the twenty-first century, and it makes people grouchy.

We don't even have time to talk to anyone. In some of these other countries, they become offended if you don't take the time to fellowship. They don't want any of this hurry stuff. We're supposed to be the ones here in America who have it all together.

I think we should go back to some basics and realize we've lost sight of a lot of things. People don't have any time for each other anymore. Kind and merciful need to be put back on our priority list.

There has to be a remnant of God's people who will draw the line in the sand and say, "That's it. I am going to live and abide by the principles of God. I don't care what it costs me personally. I don't care how hard it is on me emotionally. I am going to do what the Word of God says because I am called to be a light in a dark world and I am going to shine."

We want to do all that we can do to develop the fruit of kindness and mercy in our lives.

CHAPTER 12

PEACE — KEEPING IT

As we have seen in Galatians 5:22,23, one of the fruits of the Holy Spirit is peace. Therefore, since we are filled with God's Holy Spirit, our lives as believers should be filled with peace.

Peace must be very important; otherwise, Jesus would not have left it to us.

Jesus had peace, a special kind of peace, and He told us in John 14:27, *Peace I leave with you; My [own] peace I now give and bequeath to you. . . .* The word *bequeath* in this verse is a term used in the execution of wills. When people die, they usually bequeath, or will their possessions, especially those things of value, to the people they love who are left behind, as a blessing to them.

In this passage Jesus was going away. When He passed from this world to go to be seated at the right hand of His Father in heaven, to wait for His enemies to be made His footstool,[1] He wanted to leave us something. He could have left us anything He wanted. He could have left us any number of good things, like His power and

His Name, and He did. But in John 14:27, He tells us that He also left us His peace.

You don't leave your junk to people you love; you leave them the best that you have. So I believe that peace to Jesus was one of the most precious things He had that He could give.

PEACE IS MORE VALUABLE THAN THINGS

Nothing is worth anything if you don't have peace.

Money is no good if you don't have peace. Being famous is no good if you don't have peace. Having the most important, prestigious job in the whole company is not important if you don't have peace. How many people will spend their life trying to climb the ladder of success, and every time they go up one more rung, because of the pressure, they lose more of their peace and more of their time to spend with their family. Their whole life is consumed with the pressure and stress of trying to play all the games to keep that job. They have this position, but they have to worry about keeping it all the time. Soon, their health is falling apart, and they don't have any peace of mind.

How many people live their whole lives like that?

Some even work several jobs to acquire all the things that the world dangles in front of us, saying, "You must have this to be truly happy." They get all those "things," but they still don't have any peace.

I really believe that we are mixed up. Romans 14:17 KJV tells us, *for the kingdom of God is not meat and drink;* — it is not things — but it is *righteousness, and peace, and joy in the Holy Ghost.* As we have seen, it is knowing who you are in Christ, not living under condemnation, but having *the peace of God, which surpasses all understanding*[2] and *joy unspeakable and full of glory.*[3]

Yes, God wants us to have nice things. He wants us to wear nice clothes and drive a nice car and be able to take a nice vacation and have our needs met and be able to bless people. If God is going to bless anyone, why wouldn't it be His own children? He doesn't want the unbelievers to have all the money. But I believe that sometimes they have more sense than we do where money is concerned.

According to 1 Corinthians 1:30, Jesus is made unto us wisdom from God. In other words, believers in Jesus Christ have wisdom, yet they don't always act as if they had wisdom, especially not where finances are concerned. One cannot spend more than they make and ever enjoy exceptional living. We must follow biblical principles concerning our money. God teaches us to work hard and pay our bills. We are to be people of integrity, honorable people who are honest in every way.

GIVE AWAY WHAT YOU WANT TO HAVE

I like God's system. If you want to have more, give something away that is yours. When you get over in the area of being a giver, that's different than just giving.

A true giver goes around and looks for places to give. They are not offended when someone in ministry talks about giving. The reason is that they are doing what is right in their giving, so they don't feel pressured. They enjoy financial peace and prosperity.

PUT GOD FIRST

We have seen that God wants us to have things. But notice what Matthew 6:33 KJV tells us.

But seek ye first the kingdom of God, and his righteousness; and
all these things shall be added unto you.

Many believers miss that point, and they make a big mistake by spending their Christian life seeking money. Now there is nothing wrong with having money as long as we put God first in our life. When we do, I don't even really think that we have to spend much time believing for money.

If a farmer goes and plants his seed in good ground, he doesn't have to stand there and believe over it to grow. The seeds he has planted are just going to come up because that is the miracle of God's law of seedtime and harvest.[4] It is true that it's a spiritual law, but I'm not saying that we don't need to exercise our faith to receive. I do believe that some people just become bucket plunkers. All they do is plunk something in the bucket every time it is passed around in church without mixing any of their faith with their giving.

I believe we need to mix our faith with everything we do. But we don't have to go around from daylight until dark believing for money. God wants us to be seed minded, not need minded.

"If you have a need, don't go for it, sow for it."

SPIRITUAL POVERTY

So the kingdom does not consist of things; those are kingdom benefits. Remember that *the kingdom of God is . . . righteousness, and peace, and joy in the Holy Ghost.* It doesn't matter how much money you have; if you don't have peace, you are poverty-stricken.

There is more than one kind of poverty, but I believe that spiritual poverty is one of the worst kinds of poverty you can have. When you are in spiritual poverty, you are empty and dry and feeling dead on the inside. That means you have no joy, no peace; you don't like yourself; you are under self-condemnation all the time; you can't hear from God or feel His Presence.

When you have all of those things, you can handle anything else that comes your way. But money won't override the deadness you feel in your life. Jesus said, *Peace I leave with you; My [own] peace I now give and bequeath unto you.* I am repeating this because I want you to understand how important it is to have peace.

I found out in my own life that if I don't really understand how important peace is, I'm not going to do what I need to do to have it.

The bottom line is, you are not going to have peace just because you want peace. You are going to have peace because you operate in self-control. You will read more about self-control in a later chapter, but for now remember: Self-control is not letting negative emotions rule you. It is deciding, "I am not going to let you steal my peace." Do your best to practice self-control to remain in peace always.

Are you allowing other people in your life to steal your peace? Some people don't want to have any peace, and you are letting them take yours.

You don't need to let other people make you unhappy. If someone wants to be a grouch all day, you can't stop them, but keep your joy. Keep your peace.

At one time I was not happy in my life. I had no peace and joy, and I surely was not enjoying my life. One thing I didn't understand was that it wasn't just the big things but the little things in life that didn't go my way that were stealing my peace.

I have spent three-fourths of my life being upset. I've already lived more of my life than I have left, and I made a strong decision a few years ago that whatever time I have left, I'm going to enjoy it, and I'm going to have peace. I'm not going to become upset over this ministry or over what people think or don't think about me. I'm not going to become upset over whether people approve of me or don't approve of me, like me or don't like me, think I should be doing what I'm doing, or think I shouldn't be doing it.

Wanting to please people and make them happy is not wrong. In fact, the instruction to live in harmony and at peace with others is in the Bible.[5] But keep in mind that even if you live your life trying to make people happy, there is still going to be someone who is not going to like what you are doing.

Make it a priority to remain in peace.

IS YOUR HEART TROUBLED?

We saw earlier in John 14:27 that Jesus talked about leaving us His peace. Then He emphasized that *Not as the world gives do I give to you.* . . . Notice what He instructed us in the next part of that verse: *Do not let your hearts be troubled.* . . .

Is your heart troubled? Jesus not only commanded us in that verse to not let our hearts be troubled, but to not let our hearts be afraid and to *[Stop allowing yourselves to be agitated and disturbed; and do not permit yourselves to be fearful and intimidated and cowardly and unsettled.]*

So when you start to get upset, remember that only one thing will put an end to it. You have to stop it. You have to get hold of yourself and say, "No, I'm not getting upset."

We can choose to get upset, and we can choose not to get upset. So many times we say, "I just can't help it."

Yes, we can help it. How? I've found out that if I'm around someone I want to impress, or someone I don't want to make a fool out of myself in front of, it's amazing how I can control myself from becoming upset.

Isn't it amazing how well we can exhibit self-control when we want to impress somebody?

The truth is, we don't try to control ourselves when we're around people we don't want to impress. At those times we don't care how we act. We don't care what they think. We don't care if we hurt them, or if we're obnoxious. But we need to realize that everywhere we go, we are a witness for the One we say we serve and love.

FRUIT COMES OUT OF LOVE

Love is the first fruit of the Spirit mentioned in Galatians 5. We could have none of the other fruits of the Spirit if it wasn't for love.

How can we be patient if we don't have love? How can we have any peace if we don't have love? How could we be kind to others if it doesn't issue out of love? Why would we be good to anyone if it doesn't issue out of love?

First Corinthians 13:4 NASB begins with, *Love is patient, love is kind. . . .* If we look at the description of the fruit of the Spirit in Galatians 5:22,23 it basically says the same thing, beginning with love and ending with self-control. Love and self-control are like bookends; all the fruit of the Spirit issue out of love, but they're kept in place by self-control.

We cannot operate in peace unless our peace is linked up with love and self-control.

BE PEACEFUL ON PURPOSE

When Jesus said, *[Stop allowing yourselves to be agitated and disturbed; and do not permit yourselves to be fearful and intimidated and cowardly and unsettled]*, He was saying, "I'm leaving My peace with you, but that doesn't mean that it's just going to automatically operate. It means that I'm giving you something, a reserve that you can draw on, but you're going to have to be peaceful on purpose."

You have to understand that the devil tries to set you up to get you upset. He does his best to push you over the edge so you will lose your peace. Why? He knows that if you don't remain peaceful, your anointing won't flow. If you don't remain peaceful, you can't hear from God.

WE CAN REFUSE TO LET NEGATIVE EMOTIONS STEAL OUR PEACE.

When people lose their peace and they get emotional, they start doing all kinds of things that don't make any sense. They may say things they don't mean. They may buy items they don't really want and can't afford. They may eat food even though they aren't really hungry. Or they may be trying to quit smoking, and the devil makes them mad through some person so now they think, **I'll fix you. I'm going to go out and smoke four packs of cigarettes and three cigars.**

Who is that going to hurt except them?

You can refuse to let negative emotions rule you and not allow others to make you unhappy and steal your peace. When you start to get upset about something, make up your mind to stop it immediately. That is a good place to practice the fruit of self-control. When things start getting out of hand, self-control helps bring it back in line.

SELF-CONTROL IS SELF-RESTRAINT

When we finally reach the point of understanding what Satan is trying to do, it is almost a fun game to play.

I watch the devil now try to upset me and steal my peace, and I really enjoy holding onto my peace and knowing that I'm getting the better of him.

That doesn't mean that I don't feel upset. I'm not talking about not feeling upset in your spirit. I'm talking about controlling yourself. It's something we have to do for ourselves. Our problem is that we are always waiting for every adverse feeling to go away, and that's just not going to happen.

Yesterday morning I was trying to put my contact lens in, and I had to try seven times before I got it not to hurt. Usually I get it in my eye the first try, but yesterday it was not working for some reason. After about four tries I started laughing, and I told the devil out loud, "Sorry, devil, you're not going to steal my peace."

Today I was mixing a nutrition drink that I regularly take and as I was shaking it, it exploded and blew all over the place. I said out loud, "OK, I guess I will just clean it up and start over." I refused to lose my peace. Also, today I was making a cup of cappuccino, and I spilled the espresso while I was frothing the milk. I took a deep breath and started over without losing my peace. Satan hates it when we develop enough self-control that we can manage to stay peaceful during the storms of life. To me, this is exceptional living. I like being in control much better than having the devil in control.

BE A GOOD EXAMPLE

Sometimes we are more concerned with outward things than we should be and not nearly concerned enough about the inner life. First Peter 3:3,4 tells us: *Let not yours be the [merely] external adorning with [elaborate] interweaving and knotting of the hair, the wearing of jewelry, or changes of clothes; But let it be the inward adorning and beauty of the hidden person of the heart, with the incorruptible and unfading charm of a gentle and peaceful spirit, which [is not anxious or wrought up, but] is very precious in the sight of God.* In other words, God may like your outfit, and He may think it's cute, but He is not nearly as concerned about your outer appearance as He is with the inner condition of your heart.

It is very important that we get where we're going in peace. How can we be a witness to anybody on our job if we show up a wreck every morning? How are our children going to believe that what we preach actually works if they don't see it working in our own lives? If your children watch you throw fits three times a week, they're going to grow up and do the exact same thing that you did. If you are rebellious toward authority, don't expect your children to be submissive to you.

They see how we act in trials and tribulations, and they see how we act when the pressure is on. They see how we act when we don't get our way. They see how we act when somebody tries to correct us. They see if we are rebellious or not. And they're going to do exactly what we teach them by our actions.

We have to be a good example to people. We have to stop telling everyone else how to act, and then when we go through a test in our own lives, do just the opposite.

I remember one time I was really upset about something, and I said, "Oh, God, what am I going to do? I don't know what to do," and He said to me in my heart, "Why don't you just do what you would tell somebody else to do if they came to you with this problem?"

What would I have told them? "Well, now, you just need to calm down. You need to trust God. You need to keep your faith out there and just be patient."

It's one thing to give advice, but it's another thing to do it.

REJOICE IN THE LORD

The apostle Paul talked a lot about peace and joy. He talked a lot about righteousness because he knew what was really important in life. In Philippians 4:4 KJV he said, *Rejoice in the Lord alway: and again I say, Rejoice.*

Are you aware that Paul wrote that verse from prison? One time when I was in Rome, I visited that very prison and stood in it. Paul's bathroom-sized cell was damp and had cold, dark, stony gray walls, and it had a bad odor. I heard one report say that the prison was located where sewage from the city drained into at the time Paul was imprisoned there.

It is very possible that when Paul wrote this verse, he was standing up to his knees in sewage. How could he say to *Rejoice in the Lord*? He knew that the joy of the Lord was his strength.[6]

FRET NOT

A sure way to lose your peace is to be fretful and anxious.

Philippians 4:6,7 says, *Do not fret or have any anxiety about anything, but in every circumstance and in everything, by prayer and petition (definite requests), with thanksgiving, continue to make your wants known to God. And God's peace . . . which transcends all understanding shall garrison and mount guard over your hearts and minds in Christ Jesus.*

No message is really helpful unless some instruction is given on how to obtain the thing we need. Paul was constantly trying to teach people how to have this peace and joy. That is the end result that we all need: "Show me how I can have peace. If I've got to stop worrying to have peace, then I'm going to not worry. If I've got to stop having a negative mouth to not lose my joy, then I'm not going to have a negative mouth. Show me what to do to have righteousness, peace and joy because kingdom living is having righteousness, peace and joy in the Holy Ghost."

I think that sometimes we work a little bit too hard on the wrong things and don't work enough on the right things. We need to make up our mind that "I'm going to have peace" and start studying what the Word of God has to say about peace and start meditating on the Word about peace and watch our life.

If you watch your life, you'll be amazed when you see how many times a week Satan launches an attack against you for the sole purpose of stealing your peace.

When I finally saw that, God said to me in my spirit, "Joyce, if the devil wants your peace that badly, then there must be something pretty powerful about being peaceful."

NO STRIFE

When Jesus sent the disciples out two by two to do miracles, signs and wonders and heal the sick and tell them that the kingdom of God is near you, in essence, He said to them, "Go and find a house and say, 'Peace be unto you.' And if your peace settles on that house, then you can stay there. If it doesn't, shake the dust off your feet and go on."[7]

One time God kept bringing me to those Scriptures, and I didn't know what He was trying to get across to me. Then finally I saw it. He was trying to get me to understand the same thing that Jesus was saying to them: "I want you to go out with the anointing, Joyce, but to do that you need to have peace in the house."

In that passage, the disciples were trying to set up a base of operations, and Jesus was saying to them, "Once you find a peaceful place, that can be your base of operations, and you can go out and come back and go out and come back and go out and come back.

"If it's not peaceful, you need to do whatever you can to gain and maintain peace because it adversely affects the anointing and power of God that rests on your life."

Keep the strife out of your life — work at it. In Philippians 2:2, Paul told the Philippians to fill up and complete his joy by living in harmony.

LEARN TO SAY NO

In 2 Timothy 2:24 KJV, the Bible says that *the servant of the Lord must not strive.* We've got to keep the strife out of our lives, out of our marriages and our relationships.

It seems that it is becoming increasingly hard to get along with people. I believe the reason is that everybody's got so much pressure on them. But many times we do it to ourselves. For example, we make our own schedules.

I was complaining one day about my schedule, and God said to me, "Joyce, you made the schedule; I didn't make it. Quit crabbing to Me about it. If you don't want to do it all, then cut some of it out of your life."

We don't have to say yes to everything that comes along. We can say, "No, I can't do that. It's too much for me. I need to rest so I'm going to stay home tonight and have some peace."

I think part of our problem is pride. We don't want to ever think that anything is too much for us. We don't want to say, "If I commit to that I'll be over my head" because we might look weak.

LOVE PEACE

James 3:17 says that wisdom is peace-loving. In other words, if we're going to walk in wisdom, then we've got to love peace.

Verse 18 goes on to say, *And the harvest of righteousness (of conformity to God's will in thought and deed) is [the fruit of the seed] sown in peace by those who work for and make peace [in themselves and in others . . .].*

That tells me that Satan tries to get us upset before we go to a church service. So we're sowing seed, but it's not being sown from a heart of peace into a heart of peace.

These Scriptures say that the seed that's going to produce a harvest of righteousness must be sown by somebody who loves peace and works for peace and makes peace and keeps the peace in people who have a heart full of peace.

Years ago, I didn't have a clue about this inner life. I mean I was all caught up in the way I looked to everybody.

Jesus lives in us, and He's inside crying out, "I want some peace in the house."

We're His house,[8] and He doesn't want all that turmoil, all that worry and upset, all those negative, critical, judgmental thoughts we often have. He doesn't want us thinking negative things about our husband and family. We've got to have peace. Inner peace promotes outer peace.

JESUS IS OUR PEACE

By this point in this chapter, I hope you are getting hungry for peace.

You're not going to get this peace I'm talking about in a bottle. You're not going to get it in a pill. You're not going to get it in a needle. You're not going to get it out of some other relationship that you think you've got to have. You're not going to get it from buying yourself another thing, not a bigger house or a better car or a promotion on your job. You're not going to get it anywhere else. It must come from within.

You may have been trying to get peace every which way, but you're looking the wrong way. Jesus is our peace, and you can have peace with Him if you will accept Him into your heart and let Him rule your life.

PROTECT YOUR PEACE FROM THE PEACE STEALER

For let him who wants to enjoy life and see good days [good —
whether apparent or not] keep his tongue free from evil and his
lips from guile (treachery, deceit). Let him turn away from
wickedness and shun it, and let him do right.
Let him search for peace (harmony; undisturbedness from fears,
agitating passions, and moral conflicts) and seek it eagerly. [Do
not merely desire peaceful relationships with God, with your
fellowmen, and with yourself, but pursue, go after them!]
1 PETER 3:10,11

There is nothing that Satan works at any harder than trying to steal our peace. Jesus must have known that because He left us His peace.

MAINTAIN PEACE

When Jesus and the disciples were crossing the lake and a storm arose, the disciples panicked, but Jesus was able to stand up in the boat and rebuke the storm.[9]

You cannot rebuke the storms in your life if you have the storm on the inside of you. The disciples could not rebuke the storm because they lost their peace and were as "stormy" as the storm. But when Jesus spoke "Peace, be still" out of that well of peace that He had in Him, immediately the wind and the waves became calm.

> PEACE COMES NOT FROM A PILL, NEEDLE OR MATERIAL THINGS, BUT FROM JESUS.

We've got to have peace in our lives. To do that, we must learn to maintain peace in our relationships with God, with ourselves and with our fellow man.

We maintain peace with God by believing and trusting Him. Don't be mad at God because you prayed and what you asked for didn't happen. Don't be mad at God because your friend got healed and you didn't. Don't be mad at God because your friend got married and you didn't. Trusting God in every situation is the only way to stay in peace.

You cannot have peace without believing. According to Romans 15:13, joy and peace are found in believing. So when you lose your peace, check your believing.

Let your timing be in God's hands, as Psalm 31:15 says. You'll lose your peace if you try to make things happen out of God's timing. So stop trying to figure out what God is doing in your life and trust Him. Get out of reasoning. Get out of your brain. Stop thinking so much.

I watch people sometimes. They about drive themselves crazy trying to figure things out, like "I used to feel God all the time and now I don't feel God anymore."

I went through all that until I finally came to the conclusion, "God, no one is going to figure You out, and I'm tired of trying. You're going to do what You want to anyway, so I might as well just get in agreement with it."

It will help you tremendously when you find out that God is going to do what He wants to anyway so there is no point in trying to push against Him. You might as well just get in the flow and go with God. Having a fit is not going to make God change His mind.

When you live as long as I have, you just start getting kind of realistic about a few things. I've been around the mountain a few times. There are advantages to getting older. You finally get some sense and realize God's ways are not man's ways. Of course, you can't figure God out.

Another area in which we maintain peace is in ourselves. We do that by refusing to live in guilt and condemnation, recognizing that God is greater than all our sins.

We also maintain peace by maintaining peace with our fellow man, by not allowing strife to be a part of our relationships with other people.

CHASTISEMENT OF LOVE

When God is dealing with you, and when He is chastening you, endure it. Don't try to get away from it because God chastens us just like a loving father chastens his children.

Hebrews 12:11 NKJV says, *Now no chastening seems to be joyful for the present, but painful; nevertheless, afterward it yields the peaceable fruit of righteousness to those who have been trained by it.*

I have peace in my life now for only one reason — I've endured the chastisement of God.[10] I have let God do what He wanted to do in my life. I have let Him show me that I was prideful and haughty and obnoxious and a controller and a manipulator and hard to get along with and selfish and self-centered and that I had a big mouth. I let Him show me those things because the truth will set you free.[11] Not the truth about somebody else, but the truth about me will set me free.

It's not easy to endure that kind of godly chastisement. God won't let you off the wheel until He's ready.

It doesn't matter how many times you get tired of going around and around. God is the Potter and we're the clay, and He is going to make what He wants to out of us or it's going to be a broken mess.

Staying in bondage is harder than enduring the chastisement of God.

If I hadn't been willing to endure the chastisement of God, I'd still be back in the same old mess I was in twenty some odd years ago. I was hurting then. Yes, you have to hurt to get free, but at least you're hurting toward a victory. Your pain is not wasted. Be sure you have peace with yourself. Don't always take an inventory of everything that is wrong with you. Get delivered once and for all from guilt and condemnation. Just stop it. You're not going to pay for your sins by feeling guilty.

Believe the Word. Get washed in the blood of Jesus. Repent, admit your sins and believe that God is greater than your sins. Stop comparing yourself with somebody else all the time. Stop putting your confidence in outward things like looks, whether you're married or not, the kind of job you have, your education, gifts and talents, friends, cars, possessions.

Your worth and value are not determined by how other people have treated you and what they have said about you. Listen to what God says in His Word. Just because somebody rejected you, doesn't mean you were in the wrong. Maybe they've got a problem.

In Genesis 12:2, God told Abram (who later became Abraham) that He would bless him and make him a blessing, and I believe that He will do the same to us.

I believe that I'm a blessing everywhere I go because Jesus lives in me and that He is overflowing out of me. Not only that, I like myself because of what Jesus has done in my life; I like the new me that was recreated in Christ.[12] And that makes the devil mad too.

Apart from God I am nothing. But through Christ I can do all things.[13] I've died with Christ. We talked about dying to self earlier, and the old me is dead. Now I'm alive in Christ, a new creature. The devil really hates that. Some people don't like that kind of talk. They don't understand about being a new creature in Christ, that God restores our self-worth, and He restores our value.

Why don't you just go on over the edge right now and decide to like yourself? Just step on out and see what happens. Just jump into the ocean of God's love and say, "If You love me, God, I can love myself."

I'm talking about loving yourself in a balanced way, not a selfish, self-centered way. I finally got tired of thinking negative thoughts about myself, not liking myself, hating myself, listening to every negative person who wanted to come around and tell me everything that was wrong with me. You may have something wrong with you, but no more than anybody else. I've got a lot of things wrong with me, but no more than you've got wrong with you.

Stop letting other people run your life and be led by the Holy Ghost. Stop trying to please people all the time and be a God-pleaser, not a man-pleaser. Get the fear of man off of you. Maintain peace with yourself by refusing to live in guilt and condemnation, recognizing that God is greater than all your sins. Just let go of past mistakes and press toward the future that God has for you.

PEACE WITH OTHERS

We also maintain peace by maintaining peace with our fellow man, by not allowing strife to be a part of our relationships with other people.

Learn to recognize what strife is and get it out. Stop letting your emotions rule you. Learn to keep quiet when God says to keep quiet. Keep your opinions to yourself if you want to get along with people. Don't try to control other people; it will only steal your peace.

I used to want control over everything that went on. But I found out that trying to run the universe is a hard job. I was the great choir director of life; I had to direct everything.

When we were going out to eat, I had to direct that. If we were going shopping, I had to direct that. I had to tell everybody what to do. And I found out that people don't like to be controlled, no more than I want to be controlled.

People want to have their own opinions, their own thoughts. They want to make their own decisions. If they want my opinion, I'll give it. But, thank God, I've learned most of the time to keep my own opinions to myself.

Yes, I have that kind of personality, and I have to be careful just like everyone else does who is that way. Now, I'm not in the business of trying to control anybody because I know it will steal my peace, and I'm not giving up my peace.

RESPECT PEOPLE'S RIGHT TO BE AN INDIVIDUAL

Let people be who they are. Help your children become what **God** wants them to be, not what **you** want them to be.

For example, I think going to college is wonderful, but not every child is cut out for college. God knows what your child is going to become, and many people force their kids to go to college when they don't want to go, don't really have the anointing to go and don't even really have the brainpower to go. That doesn't mean that they're not smart or can't learn. It means they are meant for something else in life.

I have a couple of kids who probably wouldn't have made it through college with decent grades, but they're in full-time ministry now and doing great.

If somebody really has a real desire and call on their life to go to college, I'm not saying don't go to college. But I'm just saying that we can't have one set of rules for all people. I've watched parents force their kids to do that because the parents want them to go. But what do the kids want? It's not about what **we** as their parents want. It's about what **they** want. We can give our children godly advice, but we should not manipulate and control.

We need to let God run His own business.

KEEP YOUR PEACE

It is easy to lose our peace when someone hurts us. The only way to get along with people is to be generous with forgiveness. Forgive people when they hurt you. Forgive quickly when they offend you. Don't be touchy or easily offended. Concentrate on and magnify people's strengths. Don't criticize them for their faults. Don't become angry every time you don't get your way. This is very hard on relationships. Remember, we're all different. Develop an ability to adjust and adapt yourself to the different personality types in your life.

God gives us a variety of people. You may have a child who is just like you, and you don't like them because of it. Or you may have a child who is different from you, and you don't like them because they are different from you.

We can love people, but we may not like everything about them.

Jesus commanded us to love one another.[14]

I can like almost anybody now because I've learned that we're all different. But before I learned that, there were a lot of people I just couldn't endure to be around.

We always want everybody to be like us, but I've found that we need all those different people in our life. They bring balance to our life. So be a blessing to people and your relationships will be more peaceful. It's amazing how peaceful people will become with you if you're just good to them.

HEARING FROM GOD ISN'T DIFFICULT

I love the Scripture in Colossians 3:15 that says, *And let the peace . . . from Christ rule (act as an umpire continually) in your hearts [deciding and settling with finality all questions that arise in your minds, in that peaceful state] to which as [members of Christ's] one body you were also called [to live].* We are called to live in peace.

In other words, if it's peaceful, it's in; if it's not peaceful, it's out. Hearing from God is not all that difficult. Hearing from God is not about voices, it's mainly about peace and wisdom and the inner witness.

You get a witness when something is right; you feel peace about it so you do it. If you start into something, and you're going the direction you think is right, and you have peace, continue to go that way. But if all of a sudden, you lose your peace, you need to back up a few steps and say, "OK, that must not have been the way to go."

There's not one of us who can look out into our future and know everything that we're supposed to do. You hear from God one step at a time, one day at a time. As you take a step, one of the ways that you prove that you've heard from God is — does it work? Does it produce peace in your life?

ENTER GOD'S REST

Have you ever told your children, "I want it peaceful in this house. Stop running around and sit down"? I'm going to share a principle with you. The Bible says in Ephesians 2:6 that we are seated in heavenly places with Christ Jesus. We are seated — He is seated in heavenly places and we are seated with Him.

I was reading that one day and all of a sudden the Holy Ghost stopped me and really brought my attention to this fact about being seated. And I started realizing that many places in the Bible where you see Jesus, after the Resurrection, He's depicted as seated. Seems to me like it would be more powerful if He were standing in heaven.

Why was He seated?

Under Old Testament Law, when the priest went into the Holy of Holies to make sacrifices for the people's sins, to atone for their sins, he could not sit down. There was no chair in the Holy of Holies.

He had to keep moving. He had to keep working. He had to keep doing something all the time. There were bells on the bottom of his garment and if those bells stopped ringing, that meant that he had done something wrong and fell over dead. It's said they had a rope attached to him, and they couldn't even go in to get him. They'd have to drag him out.

So that was a big thing whenever they said that Jesus ascended on high and sat down as our high priest. He sat down. That said to the people, He has entered the rest of God. There was no rest of God until Jesus died for us and was resurrected from the dead.

People could not enter rest because they always had to deal with the law and sacrifices. They couldn't rest.

In Hebrews 4:3 we're told that those who have believed do enter the rest of God. There is still a rest awaiting the people of God. There's a rest that we can enter into. But you know the Bible says we have to strive to enter that rest. You have to strive to get into that rest. I like to think sometimes when I get all upset, Joyce, just sit down. Get back in your seat. Get back in your place. Stop running around trying to make something happen. Stop running around trying to get somebody to do what you want them to do. Stop trying to make that airplane come. Stop trying to make your ministry grow. Stop trying to make that person be what you want them to be. Stop trying to make things happen, Joyce. Just get in your seat and believe.

What must we do to please God? The Bible says in John 6:29, *This is the work (service) that God asks of you: that you believe in the One Whom He has sent. . . .*

Jesus wants us to have peace; joy and peace are found in believing. Why don't you enter the rest of God today about all the issues in your life? Whatever it is that you've lost your peace over, why don't you just make a decision right now, "I'm going to get my peace back because my peace is worth more to me even than getting that. . . ."

Even if you manipulate and work enough things around that you get what you want, if you don't have it with peace, it's not going to be worth anything to you.

I encourage you to say this: "I've got to have peace. I'm going to strive to have peace. I'm going to pursue peace. I'm going to crave peace and look for peace. I'm going to make whatever adjustments I have to make in my life to have peace. And when the devil sets me up to get me upset, I refuse to get upset. I'm going to hold onto my peace."

CHAPTER 13

HUMILITY — STRENGTH UNDER CONTROL

What is humility?

The opposite of pride.

What is pride?

Pride is something God hates. Pride precedes destruction and prevents promotion in our life. Pride is something that will bring you down and bring you down quickly.

There's an illustration in 1 Samuel where God promoted Saul and gave him the honor of being the first king of Israel. However, God's promotion of Saul was short-lived. He came down about as quick as he went up. God reminded Saul, "When you were small in your own sight, did I not promote you?"[1]

It's amazing how someone can have a sweet heart and a right spirit and God will promote them. Then suddenly they become a different creature. They become in their mind a person that's better than everyone else — the president of their own fan club. They begin mistreating people, putting on airs and becoming impatient with those around them. At that point, God must deal with them.

The apostle Paul said in Galatians 2:20 NKJV, *It is no longer I who live, but Christ lives in me.* It is a sign of real maturity when you can honestly say *it is no longer I* because pride is all about I. Pride is "I'm better than you, I'm smarter than you. My opinion matters, yours doesn't. Everything I do is better. I'll take care of it because I'm smarter, better."

Did you know that me, myself and I are the greatest problems that we have? We spend our time and energy admiring ourselves, simply being full of ourselves, when in reality we're supposed to be full of God and empty of ourselves — totally empty. In Luke chapter 18, there is a very good example of somebody who was full of pride and the kind of attitude they developed as a result of their pride. The spirit of pride can sneak up on you. It is always lurking around the corner waiting to get you. One of the primary ways that pride is manifested is in impatience. God showed me that impatience is the fruit of pride.

Impatience is something that happens to everyone. Do you ever get impatient with somebody who's moving too slowly in front of you? Do you become impatient with someone who doesn't understand you the first time you explain something to them?

Pride will destroy you. The best factor to determine if it is an issue in your life is if you honestly think you don't have any pride. If that is the case, that's a clear indication you've got a problem with pride. Now is not the time to think about all the proud people you know who need to read this. Pride has to do with **our** thinking. Not just the way we act. Pride starts in our own private thought life, in the judgmental thoughts that we have toward others. Such as, YOU **don't need to drive a car like that.** YOU **didn't need to spend that much on that outfit.** YOU **shouldn't be doing that with your money.**

We are so busy minding everybody else's business. The sad fact is that most of us don't do a very good job of running our own lives, let alone trying to run someone else's life. But the temptation is to get into other people's business. It's sad how much we want to get into what everybody else is doing. Why is that? I'm certainly not responsible for what you do.

God is not going to ask me about you when I stand in front of Him. That is not my worry. I can pray for you. I don't need to be judgmental and critical towards you. Those behaviors are poison to my life.

In Luke 18:9-14 Jesus tells a parable to some people who trusted in themselves — which is a manifestation of pride — and felt confident they were righteous, upright and in right standing with God. The Scripture says, *Two men went up into the temple [enclosure] to pray, the one a Pharisee and the other a tax collector.*

As you may recall, the Pharisees were revered because they were religious and the tax collectors were hated. Tax collectors were considered the wicked of the wicked. *The Pharisee took his stand ostentatiously and began to pray thus before and with himself. . . .* I love that Scripture. He wasn't even talking to God. I have found that there were times in my own life when I would pray publicly and was no more talking to God than the man in the moon. My only concern was how I sounded in front of people.

We spend way too much time concerned about what everyone thinks.

God, I thank You that I am not like the rest of men — extortioners (robbers), swindlers [unrighteous in heart and life], adulterers, the Pharisee said, *or even like this tax collector here.* He was saying, "Thank You, God, that I'm not like him; thank You that I'm so holy."

I would never pray that prayer, but that doesn't mean I've never thought it. I'm convinced that you probably have a friend in your life right now that you think you're more spiritual than they are. This would be a Christian friend who doesn't practice their spirituality the way you do. You attend early morning prayer three times a week and they don't. Your tithe even includes your birthday money and you are sure theirs doesn't.

Those Pharisees were such good little tithers. They tithed off every little mint and leaf, every little grain of spice. They wouldn't miss their tithe, but they were rotten to the core. Jesus referred to them as a bunch of whitewashed tombs full of dead men's bones.[2] Jesus had a problem with the Pharisees because they put on a good show, but they had rotten hearts.

It doesn't matter how many hours you intercede in prayer each week. If you are full of judgment for everybody else, that's a problem. It doesn't matter how many devils you rebuke and how many strongholds you try to tear down, if you are not living with the fruit of the Spirit in your life, then you are not where God wants you to be.

The parable continues, *I fast twice a week; I give tithes of all that I gain. But the tax collector, [merely] standing at a distance, would not even lift up his eyes to heaven, but kept striking his breast, saying, O God, be favorable (be gracious, be merciful) to me, the especially wicked sinner that I am!*

God would rather deal with a sinner who knows he is a sinner than a religious prune who's all soured and dried up and has no joy — a sinner who spends his life trying to make sure nobody else has any joy either.

Here's a sad story.

My daughter Sandra felt strongly that God wanted her to invite everybody in her subdivision to a recent ministry conference we had in St. Louis. She insisted, "Mom, this is the strongest I've ever felt about God leading me to do something." She followed the right lines of authority and went to the manager of their mobile home court to ask permission to put a poster by the gate and a flyer in everyone's mailbox inviting the residents to the conference.

The manager of the park is a Christian, and thought it was a great idea. They were so supportive of the idea they gave Sandra a list of names and addresses of everyone in the park. Sandra wrote a very simple letter inviting everyone to the conference.

Some of the residents got up in arms, hired attorneys and threatened to sue because the park managers distributed their names and addresses. The whole ordeal concerned Sandra because she didn't want the manager to lose his job. We all began praying and eventually the whole thing ended up blowing over. The moral to the story is that when it all came down to it, the uproar was caused by two people who stirred it up, who were also in church every time the door opens.

More trouble is often caused by hyper-religious people than any other because they can be the most judgmental. The reason for the uproar in Sandra's case was because the conference they were being invited to wasn't **their** religion, **their** church, **their** thing. They passed judgment on something they didn't know anything about. That's what religion can do to people. Religion without personal relationship with Jesus causes people to judge something — anything — without knowledge of what they are judging. When you've got a religious spirit on you, nobody can do it any way but your way. Everything is based on legalism. "If you don't do it my way, it can't be right."

Our judgmental nature prevails in our attitude. We may not say a word, but we have the attitude. Remember, Jesus lives in our hearts. More often than not, He's not pleased with some of the junk that we store in there. It's time to become real Christians, to be real people. It's time to worship Him in spirit and truth and not be a bunch of phonies. God doesn't want us trusting in ourselves.

Sometimes when we are trusting in ourselves, God has got to deal with us in a way that may seem very harsh. When a person is having a problem with pride, there's nothing that will bring them down to size any quicker than a good dose of trials. When everything is going great and the blessings are flowing and prayers are being answered — the money's pouring in, the promotions are coming and we're feeling good physically — that's when our compassion dries up.

I remember one time having a strong attitude about someone who was taking all kinds of medicine. I thought, **You don't need all that junk. Use your faith. You're just addicted to that stuff.** A few years later, I got sick, real sick, and I wasn't getting over it. I was willing to take anything the doctor would give me, even two or three bottles of it. I kept remembering how I had judged that person who had gone through similar circumstances.

It's so easy for us to know what we would do until we've got the problem.

"Well, if I were you, I wouldn't have that operation. I'd just believe God."

You don't know what you'd do if you were in their situation. Not only that, God deals with everyone individually. Early in my ministry when I had all this pride on me because I was a faith person, I had a back problem. I was so stubborn that I wouldn't even take an aspirin. I hurt for years. I had everybody laying hands on me and still was not healed. I was rebuking devils and still no healing. Then God put it in my heart to go to a chiropractor. I told God "I am **not** going. I have been believing You for all these years for healing, and I am going to be healed. I am not going to the doctor." Did you ever consider that sometimes even faith can become a pride issue? My back was getting progressively worse. I woke up one morning and couldn't walk. At that point I had no choice; I had to do something. So I went to the chiropractor.

This is the honest truth. I went wearing my trench coat with the collar turned up and my sunglasses on in broad daylight. I remember this incident because many of my friends were patients of this chiropractor. That's how I knew about him. I didn't want my friends to know I was going. I didn't want the people to recognize me at the chiropractor's office, so I tried to disguise myself somewhat. I honestly didn't realize I was trying to disguise myself. I thought I was **in faith**. Back then, my idea of **in faith** was really pride. I had no idea. Spiritual pride is the worst of the bunch. There are all kinds of pride, but spiritual pride is the one that Jesus went after. Of course, as God would have it, I ran into a lady in the waiting room that came to my weekly meetings. She looked at me rather surprised and said, "What are **you** doing here?"

Those of us who think we are better than other people spiritually will have the benefit of God orchestrating our humility. You know how to be humbled? Be humiliated.

My daughter Sandra had a problem in this area for a while. She wouldn't ask God to help her with her housework, such as ironing, because she was going to do it herself. She was always burning something, dropping something or breaking the iron. She'd get mad and frustrated and throw fits, but she was not going to ask God to help with the ironing.

Her stubbornness dug her deeper into a mess. She continued to lose her temper, and people around her were getting fed up with it. Finally, when she was ironing, she got down on her face and said, "God, You've got to help me. I can't even iron these clothes without Your help." Don't think for one minute that God doesn't want to bring us to a point of dependence upon Him. Sometimes we'll ask God to help us with the big things that we think are over our head. Here's a flash for you. Everything is over our head!

According to John 15:5 NASB, . . . *apart from Me you can do nothing.* That Scripture can be illustrated with some interesting experiences I've had. On one occasion I was trying to fix my hair and had one curl that just would not curl. The rest of my hair curled fine — my curling iron was red hot. I'd put the iron on that curl and turn it backward, take the curling iron off and that piece of hair would fall flat. I didn't know about trusting in God and leaning on God for everything. I was a self-sufficient, independent, **strong** woman. I had spent most of my life thinking I didn't need anybody because I'd been abused and was afraid to trust people. I didn't want to need anybody so this was my attitude: Who needs you? I'm just fine by myself.

I knew I needed God, but I didn't realize that I desperately needed God. I started getting this little inkling in my heart that God wanted me to pray and ask Him to help me with my hair. My first thought was, **That's stupid. I am not going to sit here and ask God to help me comb my hair. I am a grown woman, and I've been combing my hair a long time. I don't need to ask somebody to help me comb my hair. I'll try it again and spray hair spray on it because sometimes that works.** Not this time!

Finally, I conceded. "OK, Holy Spirit," I said, "would You please help me fix my hair?" I used the same curling iron and curled the same hunk of hair. However, this time when I took the curling iron off, it had this nice little curl in it. I learned a valuable lesson from that experience. If we don't do it God's way, we're not going to do it at all.

I encourage you to lean on God and ask Him to help you with all kinds of things, little things as well as big things. It honors Him when we show our dependence upon Him by asking for help.

Sometimes people put pressure on their leaders. They believe it's
OK for them to have problems, but those in
leadership are supposed to live on another
level where nothing ever touches them. That's
just not reality. I was in a grocery store not too
long ago, and a lady recognized me. She
looked surprised and said, "Well, I sure never
expected to run into you **here**! What are you
doing **here**?"

> ASK GOD TO
> HELP YOU WITH
> ALL KINDS OF
> THINGS — LITTLE,
> AS WELL AS BIG.

"Well, we eat," I responded. What a revelation. I've learned that
no matter what, I cannot live a phony life trying to meet everybody's
expectations. I've got a body just like you. Sometimes I get sick.
When I'm sick, I pray for healing. All I can do is get up and do my
very best every day.

It is certainly good to respect your spiritual leaders, but don't
put them on a pedestal and begin thinking they are more than
human. Leaders should maintain a level of spiritual maturity that
enables them to be respected and above reproach, but they are
certainly not without flaws. Preachers are people; we eat like
everyone else, sleep, go shopping, have days that we feel grouchy or
days we don't feel good physically. We need prayer and lots of it.

Sometimes prayer allows you to be healed right away.
Sometimes you've got to walk it out. I don't understand it, but I do
understand deep in my spirit that if I got every single thing that I
asked for, and every time I prayed I had a victory, I would have a
major problem with pride. None of us are equipped to have victory
all of the time without beginning to judge others. That's simply
human nature. First Corinthians 10:12 says, *Therefore let anyone who
thinks he stands [who feels sure that he has a steadfast mind and is
standing firm], take heed lest he fall [into sin].*

Sometimes we don't understand why we fail, but it's simply to keep us in our place. Dave and I have learned something over the years. If we don't get things the way we want them, we've learned to say, "We must need this," instead of saying, "Well, I don't need this." It's funny that people say just the opposite of what they should say.

I trust God that if I don't need something in my life, then He will make sure I don't have it. But if I do need it, then God will make sure that I have it. Obviously there are times when Satan attacks. It has nothing to do with something I need. It's just a demonic attack.

When you're walking with the Lord for a little while, you can tell the difference. I can tell when I am under attack. At those times I need to aggressively resist Satan and stand firm. I used to do that all the time — with everything — and not everything was from the devil. Some things were tests from God that I needed to go through. They were things that I needed to go through because I was a harsh, hard-hearted woman. I had a lot to learn. I had no compassion and God had called me to minister. You don't make a very good minister without compassion.

Compassion doesn't come by osmosis. It comes by going through things. One of the ways we get beyond judging everybody else is to have a few doses of problems ourselves. It's amazing how tender and gentle and understanding we can become when we've been in personal pain. We can empathize. Just listening to others brings back remembrance of your own pain.

Perhaps it's time to develop some sensitivity as to what other people are going through. Pride erases our sensitivity. Pride allows us just to flip out trite answers to real problems.

"I had a wreck and tore up my car."

"Well, praise the Lord anyway."

When my uncle died, it was devastating for my aunt. She married my uncle when she was fifteen. They never had children and through the years became very close. Some of my employees went to the funeral. One of my most charismatic employees in trying to comfort my aunt told her, "Well, praise the Lord." My aunt was very offended. First of all, her belief was not even in the "Praise the Lord" category. That's not meant to be insulting. It's just not the way her church would respond. It's not a phrase they would use in casual conversation and especially not to comfort someone who was grieving.

We've got to become sensitive to people. We don't know what to do sometimes for people who are hurting. You ask, "What can I do?" Sometimes the best thing you can do is just cry with them. Just grab hold of them and cry with them. Or just be there. They know you can't fix it. But they want to believe you've got some compassion and some understanding for where they're at.

There are times when the devil gets involved in a situation where he has gained a lot of authority and is able to cause tragic things to happen. That is why we should always resist the devil at his onset. If we give him a foothold, he will gain a stronghold.

There are times, too, when things happen and we don't understand the reason. You and I are messing around in the wrong territory when we start trying to figure everything out and try to put a label on it. None of us appreciate people making decisions about why we are having problems, and we should not do that to others.

You don't want people to start saying, "Well, you must not have had enough faith." Or, "There must be sin in your life." Either one of these could be the open door, but it is not our place to make decisions on that. God is the Judge, not us. People will stand before God and give an account of their life — they won't stand before us. God is the Master Who comes to receive an accounting from His stewards.

I am a faith preacher. In other words, I definitely believe in faith. The Bible says that *without faith it is impossible to please him* [God].[3] But I don't believe in pride. I think that we can get a lot of pride about our faith, which manifests in judgment of other people and why they have problems. Then, just about the time we think we have everything all figured out, God shows us that we don't have a clue about anything.

In 2 Corinthians 1:8, Paul wrote, *For we do not want you to be uninformed, brethren, about the affliction and oppressing distress which befell us in [the province of] Asia, how we were so utterly and unbearably weighed down and crushed that we despaired even of life [itself].* He goes on to say in verse 9, *Indeed, we felt within ourselves that we had received the [very] sentence of death, but that was to keep us from trusting in and depending on ourselves instead of on God Who raises the dead.*

There are numerous reasons why people experience trials. Sometimes it's demonic attack; sometimes it's disobedience. Sometimes it's a test that's stretching your faith. Everything cannot be put in one box. That's a mistake many Christians make. They attempt to put everything in a box with one universal answer. It can't be done. God is too infinite for that. His plans and our lives are too infinite. He knows what we need.

One time when I was sick I said, "What is happening? I know this isn't God; why is this happening?" God spoke to me and said, "This sickness is not unto death. It's unto life."

I knew then instinctively what God meant. He didn't have to preach me a sermon. That experience was going to allow me to be a better minister. I ended up coming out of that illness with compassion, and now I love to pray for the sick because I know what it's like to be sick.

When you've never had anything happen in your own life that brings you to your knees, then sometimes you are unable to feel what other people are going through. When we can't identify with their experience, it's very easy to judge.

Paul continues, in essence, "We were going through all kinds of stuff and it was so heavy, we felt like we didn't even want to live." He said, "The whole thing was just to keep us from trusting in ourselves."[4]

God can't use you if you're trusting in yourself. I've been doing this a long time, and I know that God allows me to go through things just to keep me in a place where He can continually use me. Anytime I start getting full of myself, God knows how to deflate my bubble. I'm glad He does. I'm glad He does because if He didn't, I would have already fallen by the wayside.

Proverbs 16:18 says, *Pride goes before destruction.* Proverbs 15:33 says, *. . . humility comes before honor.* Pride is great at hiding. It's lurking around every corner trying to get us. We must be so careful about our thoughts. You don't want to look at a friend you haven't seen in a while and say, "I just can't believe you weigh that much. You have really gained a lot of weight since the last time I saw you. What in the world have you been doing?"

Wouldn't it be better if we prayed? "God, my friend looks like they've really gained a lot of weight since the last time I saw them, and I'm sure that's not making them happy. I pray,

> HUMILITY COMES BEFORE HONOR.

God, that You'll help them lose that weight. Help them get their appetite under control. If they've got some kind of a problem in their body, God, I . . ." Why don't we pray for people instead of passing judgment? Let's start turning every one of those judgmental thoughts into a prayer. Proverbs 6:16-19 says, *These six things the Lord hates, indeed, seven are an abomination to Him:*

1. *A proud look*
2. *A lying tongue*
3. *A hand that sheds innocent blood*
4. *A heart that manufactures wicked thoughts and plans*
5. *Feet that are swift in running to evil*
6. *A false witness who breathes out lies*
7. *He who sows discord among his brethren*

Strife and sowing discord are abominations. I don't think number seven can happen unless we've got a problem with number one. I don't believe we can sow discord unless we've got a problem with pride. Discord and strife come from judgment and criticism, which come from pride. We start judging people, thinking we know more than they know; then we get into sowing discord. The world is full of that, but the Church is not supposed to be. If you don't want somebody talking ugly about you, then sow good seed.

I have to discipline my mouth just as you do. Daily, there are situations that come up where I want to get right in the middle. Sometimes I've got to say out loud, "Joyce Meyer, mind your own business. It is none of your business." An abomination is something loathsome, detestable, something dangerous, sinister and repulsive.

Humility is defined as ". . . freedom from pride and arrogance; . . . a modest estimate of one's own worth."[5] In theology, it means lowliness of mind or having a consciousness of your own defects. One of the reasons we judge other people is because we don't really have a conscious awareness of everything that's wrong with us. Therefore, we're always looking at everything that's wrong with everybody else.

"You talk too much."

"You spend too much money."

"You this and that."

Yet, we don't see anything we do.

It doesn't matter if Dave does one thing wrong and I do something else wrong. Wrong is wrong. What good does it do to judge him for the weakness he has when I've got a weakness myself?

Satan wants us to look at everybody else. Frankly, I can't do anything about Dave's weaknesses. I can pray for him, but I can't change him. I'm the only one that I can change. I can do something about me if I cooperate with God, but Satan doesn't want us seeing what's wrong with us. He's constantly holding before us everything that's wrong with everybody else, hoping we'll never get around to dealing with ourselves.

You don't need to sit around and have a bad attitude about yourself — but don't overestimate yourself either! The bottom line is that you need to get **yourself** off your mind. I need to get myself off my mind. I don't need to be thinking, **I'm worthless, I'm no good, I'm a terrible person.** And I don't need to be thinking, **I'm smarter than you, I'm better looking than you** and so on.

It's amazing the questions we ask people. If we're honest with ourselves, the questions we are asking are for comparison. We ask questions because we want to always make sure we're ahead of everybody else. Questions such as, "What kind of grades did your kids get on their report cards?" If their kids' grades are lower than our kids' we puff up. The Bible says pride is to be puffed up.[6] If you pay attention, you can feel yourself puffing.

"Oh, that's too bad."

You don't really think it's too bad. You're glad because now your kid is smarter and better. However, if their child got better grades than yours, now it's another thing.

"Oh, I'm not as good as you so now I must feel bad."

Proverbs 3:13 says, *Happy [blessed, fortunate, enviable] is the man who finds skillful and godly Wisdom, and the man who gets understanding [drawing it forth from God's Word and life's experiences].*

Galatians 5:26 says, *Let us not become vainglorious and self-conceited, competitive and challenging and provoking and irritating to one another, envying and being jealous of one another.* And Galatians 6:4,5 says, *But let every person carefully scrutinize and examine and test his own conduct and his own work. He can then have the personal satisfaction and joy of doing something commendable [in itself alone] without [resorting to] boastful comparison with his neighbor. For every person will have to bear [be equal to understanding and calmly receive] his own [little] load of oppressive faults.*

Stop comparing, stop competing and just be yourself. Be the best you that you can be and enjoy the gifts God has placed in others. Humility is free to enjoy someone else's success!

Comparison can only accomplish one of two things. It can only make you feel superior or inferior. We don't need to feel either one. We just need to be in Christ. We need to learn how to be "everything nothings." **Everything** in Him and **nothing** in ourselves. **Everything** in Christ and **nothing** in ourselves.

I believe we can do all things through Christ,[7] all things He wants us to do. And I believe that apart from Him we can do nothing.[8] Every once in a while God has to re-remind us we are nothing because if we have too many victories in a row, we start getting an attitude. That's why the apostle Paul said in Philippians 4:12, "I've learned how to be content whether I'm abased or abounding. I've learned how to be the same."

I believe Paul learned that he needed some of both. We need the warm south wind and the cold north wind to blow in our lives. If you have all good and never have a trial, or a challenge; if every prayer gets answered, and every day you feel great; if every day things work out for you, you cannot do anything but get proud and full of yourself. It is impossible to stay away from pride unless we experience some trials because trials are what bring us back into balance.

For years I didn't understand that concept, but I'm thankful God taught me because it has set me free to be content in good times and hard times.

We want to love the unlovely till somebody unlovely gets in our life. It's great to preach to people about forgiving their enemies until an enemy shows up and we've got to forgive them. How easy it is to tell people, "Now, don't be touchy. Quit being so touchy," until somebody says something to us that we don't like.

The Bible says in Romans 2:1 that the same things we judge other people for, we do.

We don't see it because we look at everybody else through a magnifying glass, but we look at ourselves through rose-colored glasses. For them there is no excuse, but we always have an excuse. "There is no excuse for you to act that way, but listen to my excuse."

Peter had a problem with pride. In Matthew 16:22, Peter rebuked Jesus. If you rebuke Jesus, you've got a problem with pride. Period. That needs no explanation. Peter had a problem with pride. He was full of himself. He thought he had a better idea than Jesus.

"Oh, no, Jesus, You must not go to Jerusalem. No, that's not the thing to do, Jesus."

Jesus had just said, "I'm going to Jerusalem."

Peter repeats himself, "Oh, no, no, that's not right."

Jesus said, "Get thee behind Me, Satan. You're in my way and an offense trying to keep Me out of the will of God."

Later on Jesus told Peter, "Satan is going to come and try to sift you, but I've prayed for you, Peter, that your faith would not fail and after you've gone through this trial that you would turn, that your faith would be strengthened and you would turn and be able to strengthen your brethren."[9] Jesus was telling Peter, "You're going to go through a little something here, but it's actually going to work out good because it's going to strengthen your faith, and then because of what you go through, you're going to be able to help other people. I've called you to minister, but there's a little defect here now that's got to get worked out."

Peter didn't believe that. He didn't say, "Oh, thank You, Jesus. Please pray for me." He said, "Oh, I would never deny You. Not me, not me, not me." When Jesus said, "One of you is going to deny me," Peter stood up and said, "Well, who is it? It certainly isn't me. I would never do that." Isn't it amazing how many things we think we would never do that we end up doing? Have you ever had that little experience? "I'd never do that." It's interesting to me that Peter was the only one of the disciples who was recognized. There were a bunch of them present, but the spotlight shone on Peter. Everyone recognized Peter after Jesus was captured.

"You're one of them," or "You're His disciple. You were with Him."

"No, I wasn't. No, I'm not. I don't know the Man." And then Peter started cussing to prove that he didn't know Jesus.[10] Why do you think that God arranged for Peter to be recognized? Because Peter needed to be humbled. God had a plan for Peter's life.

Peter loved Jesus, but he was still full of himself. He argued with Jesus on these occasions. I don't think he did it maliciously, but it always happens when someone has a spirit of pride. They just think they know more than others do and will always argue to prove they are right.

Jesus knew that Peter was useable material, but he needed some work. You might say that Peter was a diamond in the rough. He needed some polishing, he needed some time on the Potter's wheel — but he didn't see it. He was blind to his own faults just like we usually are. Jesus had to teach him a lesson, and teach him He did. Peter ended up very humbled, very repentant and very submissive after his humbling experience.

God has a plan for your life. You may not like some of the things you're going through right now. Maybe you didn't get the promotion that you thought you deserved. Maybe you are having problems with a relationship. Maybe doors are not opening that you have prayed to be opened. Trust God — He knows what you need.

I believe we need great increase in our levels of reverential fear and awe of God. It will provoke obedience rather than people doing as they please. It helps us develop humility. We become afraid to judge others harshly because we know that God teaches us in His Word not to. Reverential fear and awe is the beginning of wisdom; it helps us humble ourselves under the mighty hand of God and stop trying to do things ourselves, our own way, in our own timing. God promotes the humble, but the proud He resists.[11]

> TRUST GOD —
> HE KNOWS WHAT
> YOU NEED.

People don't have any business in a key position of leadership if they are not mature. It bothers me when I see somebody who comes along like a shooting star and overnight they're world famous. I know it's not going to last. They don't have the character to maintain that status. You may have a gift that can take you somewhere, but without the character to keep you there, you'll ultimately fall.

The Bible says to *humble yourself . . . under the mighty hand of God.*[12] You are much better off to do it yourself because if you don't,

God will be obligated to do it for you. It's a lot less painful to do it ourselves.

CHAPTER 14

JOY — YOU CAN HANDLE ANYTHING WHEN YOU HAVE THIS

The fruit of joy! What an awesome fruit. No matter what problems you have, if you have joy, joy overrides the rest of them. Just like Jesus offers us His own peace that passes understanding, He offers us joy that worldly people know nothing about. We can have joy when the circumstances of life say we shouldn't have joy. The joy of Jesus has nothing to do with circumstances.

We have a choice. We can learn to suppress or release it. I believe if we release the joy of God, it also releases an anointing that brings a refreshing in our lives. The Scripture that I've been using as a foundation, Matthew 12:33, says that you will know them by their fruit.

It's very important that we develop and operate in the fruit of the Spirit: love, joy, peace, patience, goodness, kindness, humility, faithfulness and self-control.

What is joy and what is joy based on? *Joy* defined is a shout,[1] a proclamation that can manifest in singing. *Joy* is defined as a triumph,[2] cheerful and a calm delight.[3]

When we think about joy, we may perceive that we have to be one of those bubbly people who giggles all the time, and perhaps you are not like that. I'm not like that either. I have learned over the last number of years how to have more fun. I didn't know much about fun because of the way I grew up. I have discovered how to cut loose, lighten up a little, become less serious all the time and have fun. You may need to learn the same thing. When you are serious-minded and a deep person, you can easily forget the aspect of joy and enjoying life.

Although I've learned a lot about joy, I will probably never be one of those giggly, bubbly kind of people. But I have learned to live in the midst of a calm delight. I like that part of the definition best of all.

Our joy is not to be based on our circumstances. Happiness may be based on what is happening, but not joy. Joy, a fruit of the Spirit, is like a deep well on the inside of us. It is not the fruit of our circumstance.

While I was writing this book, something happened that had not happened before. I had about 30 or 40 percent of it on my computer, and I hadn't saved it yet. A long time ago when my data processing manager set this computer up, he said to me, "You really should save everything often because you never know when you will experience a glitch."

I had never had a glitch, and all of a sudden my work disappeared. It was one little blink and it was gone. I thought it had to be in the computer somewhere. I pulled up everything I could pull up and still my message didn't appear. I finally reached one of the ladies from my office. It was over the weekend so I called her at home and said, "How do I get this back?"

She said, "If you didn't save it, you won't get it back." She said, "The computer doesn't know it was in there if you didn't save it."

My message on joy disappeared, but my joy remained.

Situations like that are not accidents. It is no different than the time a valet parking service lost my car keys. It was a test to see if I could keep my joy. I sat down and laughed aloud. You can enjoy yourself in any situation. All it takes is a decision on your part to stay in joy. Don't put your joy off for another time.

One of my favorite quotes from Alfred d'Sousa is when he said, "For a long time it had seemed to me that life was about to begin, real life, but there was always some obstacle in the way, something to be gotten through first. Unfinished business, time still to be served, a debt to be paid, then life will begin. At last it dawned on me that these obstacles were my life." This perspective has helped me to see that there is no way to happiness. Happiness is the way. So treasure every moment that you have, and treasure it more because you shared it with someone special, special enough to spend your time with, and remember that time waits for no one. So stop waiting until you finish school, go back to school, lose ten pounds, gain ten pounds, have kids, the kids leave home, start to work, retire, get married, until Friday night, until Sunday morning, until you get a new car, a new home, until your car or home is paid off, until spring, until summer, until fall, until winter, until you're off welfare, until the first or the fifteenth of the month. Decide right now that there's no better time to be happy than right now.

We serve a now God. He is not a tomorrow or yesterday God. He said, *I AM*.[4] In Hebrews 11:1, the Bible says, *Now faith is*. If I have faith about whatever may happen tomorrow, then right now I can have joy because faith is believing in God.

Romans 15:13 says joy and peace are found in believing. I cannot have joy without believing. When you lose your joy, check

> JOY AND PEACE ARE FOUND IN BELIEVING.
>
> ❦

yourself. Are you believing? It really is just that simple. Some things we perceive to be horrible problems are not as bad as we think. We go about solving them the wrong way.

Today I can believe that all my yesterdays are covered. Do you have any idea how awesome believing is? If I have made a mistake, I can come into a relationship with Jesus, stand before Him, believe He will take care of my past and provide me with a great future.

Therefore, if I believe today is taken care of, then I can enjoy right now! But if I worry about today or tomorrow, then I lose right now. If Jesus is our joy, then we can have joy in the middle of the mess. You can have joy on your way to the grocery store or vacuuming the floor. Instead of grumbling and grouching, try singing. The Bible says, . . .*be filled with the Spirit, speaking to one another in psalms and hymns and spiritual songs, singing and making melody in your heart to the Lord.*[5] It's amazing how joy begins to bubble out of your spirit when you begin to make melody in your heart unto the Lord.

Have you ever noticed if you accidentally take your mind off your problem for a few minutes, you find yourself singing or humming a song? We can shut that off by thinking about our problem again. "I shouldn't be singing; I've got a problem." A positive, joyful atmosphere filled with encouragement takes your mind off your problem, and you believe you can conquer the world. *For by You I can run through a troop, and by my God I can leap over a wall.*[6]

How can we live a positive life in the midst of a negative world? We hear negative news today. We can pray and know God will take care of us. In the meantime, I've decided I'm going to enjoy my life right now.

If Jesus tarries, I plan to be preaching when I'm ninety-five. You'll get a flyer in your mailbox that says, "Granny Meyer is coming to your town."

I keep looking at that sixty mark and I think, **In a few years, I'm going to be sixty.** That sounds different than forty or fifty, but I have joy about it. When I got over the fifty mark, I knew I was on the second side. You begin to think differently then. It made me determined to have peace and joy. *I'm going to enjoy my life.*

You will never enjoy your life unless you decide to. God gave us a free will. He said, *I have set before you life and death . . . choose life.*[7] It's like a no-brainer multiple choice test. I set before you:

A) Life

B) Death

Answer Key: Choose life

We should be able to get that. We chop our lives up in too many pieces. We want to finish this so we can enjoy that. We hurry to finish housework so we can watch a movie and enjoy ourselves. You can enjoy the housework too.

Jesus said, "I came that you might have and enjoy your life."[8] All of those things are part of life. He desires you to enjoy all of your life. He put joy in us to ensure we have joy in all things, even times when circumstances are difficult.

One of the things you can do to jump-start your joy is listen to the right kind of music. No matter how bad you feel in the morning, if you get some of the right kind of music playing, it can help you. That's a much better approach than calling a friend on the phone and complaining.

Another way to jump-start your joy is to be good to someone. It takes your mind off yourself. Our joy cannot be released if our minds remain on ourselves.

YOU CAN JUMP-START YOUR JOY.

Joy operates and flourishes in a lifestyle of giving. Preferring others has made a major change in my life.

As I mentioned earlier, I was a very self-centered woman. Although I had the fruit of joy within me, that joy was not released because the selfishness in my soul sat heavily on it. We spend too much time with thoughts about unpleasant ideas.

I don't enjoy plane rides, but I learned a long time ago if I dwell on what I don't like, then it ruins everything. So I choose not to think about it. I have learned to take things one at a time. God gives me the grace I need when I get there if I refuse to have a negative, critical attitude on my way.

You can jump-start your joy by making a decision to love your life. Dread takes all the joy out of you. God tells us not to dread anything, including our enemies.[9] People dread going to bed, getting up in the morning, getting dressed and driving to work.

Satan will try to use the spirit of dread to steal from us. "I dread to vacuum; I dread the dishes; I dread the laundry." Make a decision to love your life — all aspects of your life.

STABILITY IN DIFFICULTY

The first three years of our marriage were rough. Even though I was difficult, threw fits and wouldn't talk to Dave for days at a time, he never let me steal his joy. It made me so mad. Unhappy people work hard to make others unhappy. I believe the fact that Dave would not let me steal his joy is one of the reasons I teach on joy today.

If Dave had gotten into my pit with me, then neither one of us might have ever climbed out. Don't let people pull you down into the pit with them. You should love them, pray for them, but don't let them steal your joy.

The joy of the Lord is your strength and your witness to other people. No one wants what we have if we don't show them joy, and that joy must be perceived as "stability in difficulty." There is joy on the inside of us. We don't have to go somewhere to obtain what we need.

Once again, if you want to live positive in a negative world, then stay focused on the good things in life. I wish someone had a good news station. If every city had one good news station, more people would experience joy. Instead, you see people killing each other and every news station in town covers it. That's the devil magnifying evil.

I believe my Bible, and in Romans 12:21 it says that we overcome evil with good. Good is still stronger than evil. Light remains greater than darkness, and life is stronger than death. We have all it takes to live the right kind of life. I'm determined if everybody around me wants to be a grumpy, grouchy mess, then I'm going to pray for them and hope they change. I will not climb into their pit with them. I will keep my joy. Make a decision not to go down the drain with everyone else who wants to go.

STAY FOCUSED ON THE GOOD THINGS IN LIFE.

RIGHT RELATIONSHIP

Joy is based on a *right* relationship with God. Many people have a relationship with God, but it's not a right relationship.

Romans 14:17 KJV says, *For the kingdom of God is not meat and drink; but righteousness, and peace, and joy in the Holy Ghost.* I believe that's a progressive statement. If I start at the bottom, I can have joy. We must maintain a **right** relationship with God and know who we are in Christ, which causes us to experience peace and joy. I have to know that I've been made the righteousness of God in Christ.[10] I can't have joy if I continually take inventory of everything wrong with me.

We all do some things wrong, but we also do many things right. You are reading this book today, and that's right. If we will keep our focus on the right things, I believe they will override and overcome the wrong things. In fact, I don't think there is any other way to get out of trouble.

I don't think it's possible to get out of trouble if you're not positive. Maybe your problems are not nearly as deep as you think they are. Maybe you have become negative and simply having a more positive attitude would help.

If you grew up in a negative atmosphere where everybody around you was negative, you may not realize how negative you are. It's time to get to know positive people; then you will begin to think and speak positively.

There's nothing negative about God. Amos 3:3 KJV says, *Can two walk together, except they be agreed?* In order to walk with God we must come into agreement with Him. God says He loves you, so you need to **say** He loves you. God says you have worth and value. You need to **say** you have worth and value. God says if you're in Christ Jesus then you've been made the righteousness of God, so you need to **say,** "I've been made the righteousness of God in Christ." Choose to **say** what God says about you.

We have to be quick to repent to maintain that right relationship. Hidden sin and sin we refuse to confront cause major problems in our soul and will steal our joy. We can't hide from it. If our conscience is heavy, we know it. One of the best ways to maintain your joy is to keep your conscience clean.

We are assured of a clean conscience by doing everything right, by admitting our sins, repenting and receiving forgiveness. If you offended somebody, go apologize. If you did not treat somebody right, ask for forgiveness. It is better to humble yourself and apologize than to keep that heaviness. There is no harder pillow to lay your head down on at night than to know that you disobeyed God that day and you haven't taken care of it.

Psalm 32:1-4 says, *Blessed (happy, fortunate and to be envied) is he who has forgiveness of his transgressions continually exercised upon him, and whose sin is covered.*

Blessed (happy, fortunate and to be envied) is the man to whom the Lord imputes no iniquity and in whose spirit there is no deceit. When I kept silence [before I confessed], my bones wasted away through my groaning all the day long. For day and night Your hand [of displeasure] was heavy upon me; my moisture was turned into the drought of summer. Selah!

David said, "Before I confessed, I felt like a bunch of old, dry, dead bones, and Your hand of displeasure was heavy on me." That is a great description of what it feels like when God's dealing with you and you refuse to submit to Him.

David continues in verse 5, *I acknowledged my sin to You, and my iniquity I did not hide. I said, I will confess my transgressions to the Lord [continually unfolding the past until all is told] — then You [instantly] forgave me the guilt and the iniquity of my sin. Selah!*

This is the central theme of the Gospel of Jesus Christ. He forgives our sins, and we can be continually forgiven of our sins.

Many people ask God to forgive their sins and then they don't receive forgiveness, but try to work their way back into God's good graces.

In verse 6 David says, *For this [forgiveness] let everyone who is godly pray — pray to You in a time when You may be found; surely when the great waters [of trial] overflow, they shall not reach [the spirit in] him.* He says that if we will pray for this forgiveness and walk in this forgiveness, we will have such strength of spirit that when the great waters of trial overflow in our lives, they won't be able to get to us.

Verse 7 continues, *You are a hiding place for me; You, Lord, preserve me from trouble, You surround me with songs and shouts of deliverance.* . . . He tells us right in the middle of trouble God surrounds us with songs and shouts of deliverance.

Sometimes we don't make enough noise to scare the devil off. The minute you begin to feel depressed and oppressed you should shout aloud, *Hallelujah!* Watch and see what happens. Oppression and depression can't stay near us when we give shouts of joy. The devil will tell you that you're acting stupid. I would rather act foolish for God than for the devil. Depression and a sour, sad face and attitude are acting foolish for the devil. It is exactly what he wants you to do. Perhaps shouting, *Hallelujah!* when you're in a room all by yourself seems foolish, but at least you are doing it in obedience to one of God's principles.

There are things that we can do to overcome our problems, but often we don't want to do them. When we feel down, we honestly don't feel like listening to music because there's a certain negative edge in your old man that wants to wallow in it. We need to shake it off! We are new creatures in Christ![11]

We are equipped with what we need to be more than conquerors, but we have to **choose** to operate in what we have. Joy is a daily choice, and you must not allow the devil to deceive you by swallowing the lies that this may work for everyone else, but your problems are too big for it to work for you. That is not true. That's a lie.

Jesus said in John 16:33, *In the world you have tribulation. . . .* His answer to it was, *. . . be of good cheer . . . I have overcome the world.*

Maybe you have had many negative things happen in your life. God wants you to know your time of mourning is over! It's time to stop grieving over what you've lost.

There is a period of time for mourning, but there is a time to shake it off and move forward in your life.[12] Maybe you lost someone you loved. Maybe you lost your job, a favorite possession or a relationship. I have lost a lot of things, and I know what it's like to hurt. The answers are biblical answers found in the Word of God.

Nehemiah 8:8,9 says, *So they read from the Book of the Law of God distinctly, faithfully amplifying and giving the sense so that [the people] understood the reading. And Nehemiah who was the governor, and Ezra the priest and scribe and the Levites who taught the people said to all of them, This day is holy to the Lord your God; mourn not nor weep. For all the people wept when they heard the words of the Law.*

Apparently, what they heard seemed to them like more than they could handle, and it caused them to weep. In verse 10 it says, *Then [Ezra] told them, Go your way, eat the fat, drink the sweet drink, and send portions to him for whom nothing is prepared. . . .* Right in the middle of this he reminds them, "And be sure to be a giver." Even in our trials we should reach out to others in need.

In verse 10 he is saying to eat the fat, drink the sweet, send portions to those who don't have as much as you do. Reach out and help somebody else. *For this day is holy to our Lord. And be not grieved and depressed, for the joy of the Lord is your strength and stronghold.*

A stronghold is a place where you can be protected from your enemies. Joy protects you from the enemy. Your enemy doesn't like joy, but prefers depression, despair, discouragement, disease and distress. Jesus is our glory and the lifter of our heads.[13]

The Israelites were very dependant upon Moses. He did their praying, believing and repenting. All they did was wander around and act foolish. When Moses died, the Israelites mourned.

And the Israelites wept for Moses in the plains of Moab thirty days; then the days of weeping and mourning for Moses were ended.[14] When someone died, they were allowed thirty days to mourn. After that, they had to get over it and go on.

God is never depressed about problems. He always has a new plan. When one thing ends, God has a plan for the next thing that we can do. When we are disappointed, we don't have to become discouraged and depressed — we can become re-appointed. No matter what has finished in your life, God is not finished with you. If He was finished with you, you wouldn't be here.

> WHEN ONE THING ENDS, GOD HAS A PLAN FOR THE NEXT THING THAT WE CAN DO.

You may think you were a mistake or that you have no value or purpose. If you feel that way, it's because of your own way of thinking, not what God would do with you if you gave Him a chance.

Joshua 1:1,2 says, *After the death of Moses the servant of the Lord, the Lord said to Joshua the son of Nun, Moses' minister, Moses my servant is dead.* They already knew that Moses was dead because they had been mourning him for thirty days. God is making an emphatic statement.

The Bible says that God wants to turn your mourning into joy: *Weeping may endure for a night, but joy cometh in the morning.*[15]

Ecclesiastes 3 says there's a time to weep and a time to mourn, a time to laugh and a time to play. There's a time for everything. We'd be cold-hearted and lacking compassion if we lost something and felt nothing. But after a period of time, you must let go of what lies behind and press forward. If you don't let go, the past will destroy your future.

It may be hard to forget. When you're not doing anything, you think about the past. When you move forward to something new, you have something new to put your life into, something new to think about. It's a decision only you can make.

Multitudes, multitudes in the valley of decision, Joel shouted.[16] Make a decision to have joy now. Decide to shake off the past and go forward. Your time of mourning is over.

We should enjoy everything we are doing right now and refuse to mourn the past — "Well, I wish, I wish . . . . If only I would have, and if only I wouldn't have."

God said, *Moses My servant is dead. So now arise [take his place], go over this Jordan, you and all this people, into the land which I am giving to them, the Israelites. Every place upon which the sole of your foot shall tread, that have I given to you, as I promised Moses.*[17] He's saying, "Let go of the past and take new ground. Every place the sole of your foot treads, I will give it unto you. Go forward and don't look back."

We don't always have to go back and try to do what we once did. We can go on to the new assignments God has for us. I believe God always saves the best till the end. My life has been progressive. It keeps getting better and better and better. I don't plan to reach some peak and then go downhill from there.

First Samuel 16:1 says, *The Lord said to Samuel, How long will you mourn for Saul, seeing that I have rejected him from reigning over Israel? Fill your horn with oil, I will send you to Jesse the Bethlehamite. For I have provided for Myself a king among his sons.*

Saul was Israel's first king and he went sour. God didn't get depressed, He got a new king. Samuel was so disappointed because he had worked with, prayed for and prophesied to Saul.[18] Samuel had ministered to and believed in Saul.

When we believe and invest our time in someone and then they go sour, sometimes we become sour with them. We feel like we can't trust anyone again because we might be disappointed.

I think Samuel had that same attitude. Sometimes you get tired of working with people. We sometimes expect more out of Christians than we can ever receive. I am not going to have a sour attitude. God's horn is always full of fresh oil.[19] If one person won't do what's right, and I keep my eyes on God, He will find me two more who are better than the one I lost.

Today is the day to go forward. Remember, joy can override all your discouragements and disappointments in life. Jesus gave us His joy, and the joy of the Lord is our strength. All it takes is a decision. **Choose joy!**

CHAPTER 15

SELF-CONTROL — MAKING THE RIGHT CHOICES

I n the world today, Christianity doesn't have a great reputation. The attitude people have about Christians can be painful sometimes because they see us from the world's perspective. But another part of it is Christians don't always live up to what they say they believe.

We aren't perfect, but we can all come up higher. We make mistakes, and there is always someone who will say, "You're a hypocrite," if you don't behave perfectly. The Bible very plainly tells us we will be known by our fruit.

We can become overly concerned about gifts. I spent many years praying about the gifts of the Spirit in the early days of my ministry. I wanted the gifts of healing, the word of knowledge and the word of wisdom, as well as all the other gifts. The Bible says the gifts of the Spirit are given for the good and the profit of all.[1]

Many times we seek gifts to make us look good and even compete over the gifts of the Spirit. People will ask, "What's your gift?" I remember in the seventies and eighties, if you hadn't located your gift yet, then you were nothing.

As mentioned earlier, after a period of time in ministry and spending time praying about the gifts of the Spirit, God finally spoke to me one day, and He said, "Joyce, you hardly ever pray about the fruit of the Spirit. You just want the gifts." He said, "If you had been praying about the fruit, you would probably already have the gifts and the fruit."

If we're only interested in gifts, then the gifts we have will never reach their full potential.

Remember, Jesus said, *I give you a new commandment: that you should love one another. Just as I have loved you. . . . by this shall all [men] know that you are My disciples, if you love one another.*[2] As we have seen, love should be our number one priority. Love is the fruit of the Spirit and all the other fruit comes out of love.

In Galatians 5 love is the first one mentioned and self-control is the last one mentioned. I believe love and self-control are like the bookends that hold everything else in place.

We will not operate in any of the fruit of the Spirit without self-control. The fruit of the Spirit is not about how we **feel**, but about what we choose to **do**. If you wait to feel like being nice, then you may hit it occasionally on one of your good days, but most likely you will experience quite a few days when you don't feel like being nice. You can be saved, full of the Holy Spirit and operate in many gifts, but there still will be times when you feel like smacking someone upside the head.

The Bible has much to say about self-control. Self-control is a fruit of the Spirit that we are to develop and choose to operate in. God gives us self-control so we can discipline ourselves. Without self-control, we cannot have the things that we desire.

I had a desire for this ministry. If I had not developed the fruit of self-control in my life, I could not do what I do today. You must discipline yourself to study, to pray and to do things when you don't feel like doing them.

You have to discipline yourself to do things you find distasteful. Preaching from the pulpit is the most minor part of what I do. I preach one or two days a week and study sometimes eight and ten hours a day. While I am doing that, there are people who go out to dinner or play golf. If you're going to do something, you have to exercise self-control and stay committed by learning to say no to things that you want to do so that you can prove successful.

The devil will lie to you. He'll tell you, "You don't have a life," but if you don't fulfill the call of God on your life, you will be miserable. I prefer to have inner fulfillment to outer fulfillment. When I lay my head down at night, I want to know I have been in God's will all week.

It takes self-control. We have to discipline our thoughts. We have to discipline our mouth. Maybe you don't think you have any discipline. Yes, you do! If you are saved, you have discipline and self-control within you. You may not have developed it, and you may not want to use it, but it is there. Second Timothy 1:7 says that God did not give us a spirit of fear. *The Amplified Bible says, For God did not give us a spirit of timidity (of cowardice, of craven and cringing and fawning fear), but [He has given us a spirit] of power and of love and of calm and well-balanced mind and discipline and self-control.*

> IF YOU ARE SAVED, YOU HAVE DISCIPLINE AND SELF-CONTROL WITHIN YOU.

Your mind has everything to do with it. Once you really set your mind to something you **know** you should do, no devil can keep you from doing it. Your will is stronger than demons. I'll give you an example.

I battle with three to seven pounds of extra body weight. Over the years, I would lose it and then gain it back. We all have our ideal weight that we'd like to weigh. Maybe you wish all you had to deal with was five pounds. That may sound ridiculous, but whether it's two pounds or a hundred pounds, the principle is the same.

Over the last three years it seemed to me like it became more and more difficult to keep that extra five pounds off. I have friends who can eat more than I can, and they're still smaller than I am! We can complain about our metabolism, but that doesn't make it work better. Feeling sorry for myself doesn't help me do what I need to do.

My friend weighs ninety-five pounds. She weighed ninety-three pounds for the first twelve years I knew her. It would be difficult for me to feel sorry for her; she gained a whole two pounds. She eats as much as I do. I passed up ninety-five pounds a **long** time ago. I just went back and forth. It seemed like I could not lose this weight. I made up excuses for not losing weight. "I work too hard on the road to deal with all that," I said.

I was in my television studio a couple of weeks ago, and I put on a suit that looked real nice a year ago, but it didn't look so nice anymore. When I looked at myself in that suit, I said, "That's it. I'm losing this weight." I learned a valuable lesson from that experience. I had been playing around with it. I wanted to lose it, but I didn't want to give up some of the things I was eating. It's one thing to say you're going to lose weight. It's another thing to continue to say it when you are hungry. Two days later, I was sitting at my computer working and hunger pangs hit me so hard that I thought I was going to fall out of the chair.

My stomach actually hurt. I said to my body, "Shut up. You are not getting anything until lunch. I don't care how you feel or how big a fit you throw. Shut up. You're not eating." Immediately that feeling lightened up to the point where it was OK. I got it off my mind.

We need to talk to ourselves more often in the right way. We normally say, "I'm starving, I'm starving. I can't stand this. I've got to eat. My blood sugar is falling. I'm going to faint."

After a few weeks, I'd lost what I wanted to lose and it proved to me that if you really desire to make a change, you can. I had been fighting this for three years. In a few weeks of real discipline, it was taken care of.

I do want to say that I realize there are people with chemical imbalances, and it is impossible for them to lose weight until things are brought into balance in their bodies. I also know as we get older our metabolism slows down, and maintaining the same weight becomes more and more difficult. Each person must find what works for them, but whatever that is it will require self-control, which is a fruit of the Spirit that God has graciously given to us.

Even if a chemical imbalance exists, it will probably take changing the eating habits to bring correction. Good quality food helps produce good quality results in our bodies. I cannot eat a lot of things that my mouth would enjoy tasting simply because they have no real nutrition in them, and I cannot afford to waste my calories. Often when others are eating desserts, I must choose to say no thank you. God said in Deuteronomy 30:19, *I have set before you life and death . . . choose life. . . .* I try to remember this each time I sit down to a meal. I can make choices that will enhance my health, but I can also make choices that will hurt it. I have a wonderful call on my life, and I intend to finish what God has called me to do. I need to be healthy to do that; therefore, I simply cannot do everything everyone else does, nor can I do everything I might feel like doing.

I thank God for the fruit of self-control. We would be in an irreconcilable mess continually in our lives if God had not equipped us with this wonderful, helpful fruit. Don't ever say, "I just have no self-control." Begin to say what God's Word says about you, "I have the fruit of self-control, and I am able to do whatever I need to do in any situation because God is my strength."

We must learn to recognize when we **begin** to let things slip. Although you may be strong-willed and very disciplined, the devil will still try to deceive you. He is looking for an area in your life where you are not making firm decisions. We must be watchful to set our minds in agreement with what we know God wants us to do. You cannot let any negative double-minded thoughts steer you from your goal.

It takes a commitment to do whatever it takes. Here is another example. We needed to remodel some of the inside of a previous house. We had lived in it for ten years. The carpet was worn, we needed a few new drapes and some of the blinds had kinks in them from people peeking out through them. We needed new wallpaper and paint. There is no bigger mess than trying to remodel a house while you're living in it.

I felt like God put it in my heart to do it, but I didn't want to do it. I kept going back and forth between "Should I do it?" and "I don't want to do it." I made a decision and got a new mindset. "The mess will only last two months; then I'm going to love the results." Many of us want results, but we don't want the mess that comes with it. We want the gain but not the pain. We want to look good but we don't want to discipline ourselves in our eating habits.

If we play around too much with stuff in our mind, we become double-minded. Yes, I will. No, I won't. I don't feel; I don't think; I don't want.

Everything in life takes quality decisions, self-control and discipline to make it happen. Cleaning your house, losing weight, not spending more money than you should, maintaining peace—all require self-control. God is not going to send angels to vacuum our floors no matter how much we rebuke the dirt in our house. It will not go away unless we clean it!

Self-control is the art of controlling oneself. I think it is kind of interesting that most people don't want to control themselves, but they want to control everyone else. People that control and manipulate, don't usually control themselves. It is necessary that we understand it's the fruit of self-control.

It is virtually impossible to show forth the other eight fruits of the Spirit unless we walk in self-control. How can we remain peaceful in the middle of an upsetting situation unless we exercise self-control?

Self-control allows us to be patient when we feel impatient. You don't wait to feel patience, but choose to be patient. I can't be impatient just because I feel like it. It is not pleasing to God. I want to please God. I want to be like Christ. I want to display the fruit of the Spirit because I want other people to become hungry for what I have.

Feelings are your number one enemy. People tell me how they feel more than anything. "I feel God; I didn't feel God. I feel like giving; I don't feel like giving. I don't feel like going to that meeting. I'm going to wait and see how I feel in the morning before I make a decision." If that's your motto in life, then you can stamp disaster across your life and go on. You will not experience victory unless you discipline yourself and make decisions to do what you know you should do.

People commit to do something when they're in the height of emotions, and then when all the emotional stuff is over, they don't feel like doing what they said they would do. This is why we have such a lack of integrity in our society today. People can't trust each other to keep their word. They are suspicious of everyone. We lack

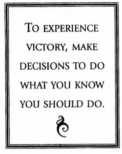

honor, integrity and excellence. People choose to be mediocre, and I'm personally very tired of it. I'm hungry for excellence.

The world may choose to be that way, but we are not in the world and not of the world. As sons and daughters of the Most High we should imitate Him.[3] He is excellent and full of integrity. He keeps His Word.

How can I exercise humility without self-control?

When Dave first began to tell me to do things, it was just like the Fourth of July going off on the inside of me, and it wasn't a party either. I have gotten better over the years.

Every time you discipline yourself to do the right thing, the next time is a little bit easier. Whatever we exercise becomes the strongest. If I exercise my temper, then my temper becomes the strongest. If I exercise impatience and vent impatience every time I feel impatient, then impatience grows stronger and stronger.

As born-again Christians we have the fruit of the Spirit in us, but if we don't purpose to exercise it, all these other things that oppose it will stay stronger. That produces carnal Christians who are not walking in the Spirit because they refuse to exercise the fruit of the Spirit, including self-control.

The Holy Spirit leads us to operate in the fruit of the Spirit. He's not just going to lead me to prosperity, success and everything else I want if I refuse to allow Him to lead me through the other things I need in my life.

Choose to stop saying, "I just don't have any discipline or self-control." If in the natural you are the most undisciplined person in the whole world, begin to say at least fifty times a day, "I have a spirit of discipline and self-control. I am disciplined; I am self-controlled. I do not **do** what the devil desires, but only what God tells me to do. I have a strong will and my will is turned in God's direction. And I am **not** going to do what I feel like doing anymore."

I learned how to talk right to myself. You can choose to talk to yourself in such a way that will help you. We can say wrong things that cause us trouble. The devil puts wrong thoughts in our mind and then we speak those wrong things out. "I can't control my appetite." Don't say that. Say, "I eat what is good for me. I don't just eat what I don't want. I don't care how good the food looks or who else is doing it, I refuse to do what the real me doesn't want to do."

Sometimes we think things like appetite have nothing to do with our spiritual lives. Yes, they do! Grasp the revelation: If we are not disciplined in other areas of our lives, then we won't become disciplined in spiritual things.

We have more than one appetite. Sometimes people have such an appetite for things that it controls them. We must be cautious that our appetite for some things like merchandise, entertainment or even sex stays balanced.

Self-control is to live in moderation. I think we must be careful about extravagance. There is a difference in prosperity and just seeing how extravagant you can be. God is not wasteful. Avoid extremes and stay within reasonable limits. Self-control is mild or calm restraint in actions and in speech.

We need to think about our mouths. James 3:2 says that if any man can control his mouth then he can control his entire nature. The Bible says that no man can tame the tongue.[4] If we work with the Holy Spirit enough to get our mouth under control, every other area of our lives will be under control.

If we don't have self-control, our emotions will rule us and we will lead miserable lives. I remember when a spirit of self-pity controlled me. Every time Dave didn't do what I wanted, I'd have a pity party, pout all day, cry, carry on and be miserable. It doesn't change anything. Only God can change the circumstances in our life. Throwing fits will not change it.

Acts 24:24 and 25 say, *Some days later Felix came with his wife Drusilla, who was a Jewess; and he sent for Paul and listened to him [talk] about faith in Christ Jesus. But as he continued to argue about uprightness. . . .* Now when they say *argue* it doesn't mean Paul was arguing. He was pressing his point.

The Amplified Bible says, *. . . uprightness, purity of life (the control of passions). . . . Felix became alarmed and said, Go away for the present; when I have a convenient opportunity, I will send for you.*

Felix said, "I don't want to hear this stuff right now. I'm willing to listen to faith if you're going to tell me how I can use my faith to get what I want, but if you're going to talk about using your faith to go through trials then go away and come back another time. This is not a convenient day. I don't mind you talking about prosperity. I don't mind you talking about my healing, but do you have to talk about self-control?"

It doesn't matter what kind of problem we have in our lives. Self-control comes into play in every area of our lives. There are certain messages in the Bible that fit everything and this is one of them.

If you need self-control in any area of your life, don't put it off until another time. There is no time like the present. First Timothy 3:1,2 says, *The saying is true and irrefutable: If any man [eagerly] seeks the office of bishop (superintendent, overseer), he desires an excellent task (work). Now a bishop (superintendent, an overseer) must give no grounds for accusation but must be above reproach, the husband of one wife, circumspect and temperate and self-controlled. . . .* I find it interesting that one of the first qualifications for leadership is self-control.

Verses 2-4 continue, *[he must be] sensible and well behaved and dignified and lead an orderly (disciplined) life; [he must be] hospitable [showing love for and being a friend to the believers, especially strangers or foreigners, and be] a capable and qualified teacher, not given to wine, not combative but gentle and considerate, nor quarrelsome but forebearing and peaceable, and not a lover of money [insatiable for wealth and ready to obtain it by questionable means]. He must rule his own household well, keeping his children under control. . . .*

It really disturbs me when I see a two- or three-year-old child hitting his parents. Many parents today are afraid to spank their children in public because of the way the laws read.

If you have a strong-willed child, I suggest you become more strong-willed than he is. If your child acts improperly in public and you don't feel you have the freedom to properly correct him where you are, you can always consider leaving the store or wherever you may be, taking him to the car or home if need be and bringing the correction needed.

I am certainly not advocating beating or abuse, but a good spanking in the proper place never hurt anybody who needed it. Any child who hits their parents needs a good spanking. I think one of the reasons why God so amply padded our backsides was so we could absorb spankings when we needed them.

If you will be disciplined to discipline your child, especially at those times when it might be inconvenient to do so, you will quickly win the war. The child will realize there will be consequences for wrong behavior. I feel like many people don't discipline themselves to discipline their children — this is tragic.

If you correct your child and say, "Now, you're going to stay in the house for a week," then as the parent, you have to suffer through that. Some people let their kids do whatever they want because they don't want to go through what it takes to stand firm.

I have to discipline myself to discipline employees who require correction. I certainly don't feel like doing it, but I would not have this ministry if I didn't take care of things that cause strife in my office.

We are not being good stewards over what God has placed in our care if we refuse to bring discipline when it is needed. Lack of proper godly confrontation gives the devil a foothold, and he will move on to a stronghold if he isn't stopped. We must remember that the devil is aggressive, and we will not defeat him with passivity.

You've got to do things you don't want to do if you want to be a success. If you want to be all that you can be, then you must do some things you don't want to do. It must not be an occasional, once in a while occurrence. It must be a regular part of your life all the time.

> TO BE SUCCESSFUL, WE NEED TO DO THINGS WE DON'T WANT TO DO.

I believe that Christians should pay their bills. That takes discipline. It takes discipline to purchase only what you can pay for. You may have gotten into a financial mess before you got saved. I'm not trying to condemn you, but I do encourage you to discipline yourself now.

I find it interesting that it is difficult for some churches to obtain loans because they have such a terrible reputation for not paying their bills. Often people don't want to work with churches because of their bad reputation. Christians certainly should have a good reputation in this area as well as all other areas. There are times when people say they are taking a financial step in "faith." In other words, they are buying something and believing that God will provide the money to pay for it. There may be times when God asks us to take a step of faith, but if He does, He will always pay the bills. You must discern the difference between God asking you to take a step and you taking one and asking God to pay for it. God pays for what He orders, but He does not pay for everything we decide to buy. We must learn to wait on things we want. Our society is one of instant gratification, and the "buy now, pay later" plan that is so popular helps us avoid disciplining ourselves and waiting.

Second Corinthians 5:14 says that the love of Christ constrains us or controls us. I do many things for the love of God that I would not do for any other person on the face of this earth. There are many times when Dave and I have a heated discussion and I shut my mouth for Jesus. I smile and say, "Yes, Honey."

There are many areas that I don't want to discipline myself in, but I do it because I love Jesus. To be honest with you, that's when I finally quit smoking. Smoking is not only bad for your health, it has a controlling effect. Paul said that he would not allow anything to control him, and I believe that is a good rule to live by. We want to please God, but we're not always willing to suffer to please God.

We want to do what God tells us to, if it doesn't cost us too much or inconvenience us. We must stop walking by how we feel and do what we know is right. The Bible says to be not weary in well doing, or in doing what you know is right, for in due season you shall reap if you faint not.[5]

Luke 6:35 says, *But love your enemies and be kind and do good, [doing favors so that someone derives benefit from them] and lend, expecting and hoping for nothing in return but considering nothing as lost and despairing of no one; and then your recompense (your reward) will be great.* . . . No one wants to love their enemies. The Bible even says if someone borrows something from you and doesn't bring it back, then don't feel you lost anything. Say, "Well, I'll just give it to you."

Refuse to allow bitterness into your heart. We were on a large television network five years ago that was bringing in the most financial support. We had been faithful to pay our bills on time and had done everything they asked us to do, when suddenly they took us off the air. They changed their programming and took all the religious broadcasting off at that hour of the morning.

It hurt me so bad. I felt robbed because we had done what was right. We had a contract. They didn't pay heed to the contract and for a few days I cried. As I sat in church one Sunday morning, my pastor talked about giving and it hit me like a ton of bricks. God said to me, "You can give that station as a seed or you can feel like you've been robbed. And if you give it as a seed, then I'll give you a harvest."

That word was strong in me. I got up in church and shared it. I made a decision that day. I refused to become bitter and resentful and sowed it as a seed. Now I am on that same network every day, not once a week, and at a better time than I had before. **They** asked **me** to come back on. My reward doesn't come from people. It comes from God.

In Ephesians 5:22, the Bible talks about a subject we don't like to hear: *Wives, be subject (be submissive and adapt yourselves) to your own husbands.* I don't like the words **adapt** and **submit**. Most of us want our own way. Here's the kicker: *as a service to the Lord.* We do it because we love God. It takes self-control.

Colossians 3:23 says, *Whatever may be your task, work at it heartily (from the soul) as [something done] for the Lord and not for men.* If you have served in the church for five years and no one has said thank you, don't quit because they didn't thank you. Only quit because God tells you, "I want you to quit now."

Yes, we all need appreciation because we need to be encouraged. If people do not appreciate you, they are wrong — but two wrongs don't make it right. If you are on a higher level and someone sinks to a lower level, how is it going to help you if you let them pull you down? Choose to stay up and become determined not to sink with them. That's when God promotes you.

In Job 32:17-20 Job said that he was full of words to the point of feeling like he was going to burst open, but he said, *the spirit within me constrains me.* With everything that he was going through Job exercised self-control. His friends came against him. He was blamed and accused but he constrained himself.

You can be full of words to the point where you feel like you're going to burst, and the spirit works hard to try to constrain you. Restraining ourselves is biblical.

In 1 Samuel 3:13, Eli did not restrain his sons who were sinning, and a curse came on his whole house. His sons died in battle. The ark of God was captured, and Eli fell over dead. All because he would not make his sons obey.

Proverbs 1:2,3 says, *That people may know skillful and godly Wisdom and instruction, discern and comprehend the words of understanding and insight, receive instruction in wise dealing and the discipline of wise thoughtfulness, righteousness, justice, and integrity.* The Bible tells us in thoughtfulness and giving, we still have to use wisdom and discipline because if a person has a gift of mercy, they can give to someone to the point where they hurt them.

You can hurt your children by doing too much for them and making everything so easy for them that they never have to believe for anything. Dave has to restrain me once in a while regarding our children because I would give them the bank. As a mother, I want to bless them, but if I do too much, I can actually hurt them.

My son, do not walk in the way with them [sinners]; restrain
your foot from their path.
PROVERBS 1:15

I need to discipline myself not to hang around the wrong
people. If you spend time with a gossip, you're going to gossip.
Because spirits are transferable, if you sit with a negative person,
then you're going to be negative. If they don't get what you've got,
you're in danger of getting what they've got.

That is exactly why when you are saved you must be very careful
about just going back and hanging out in all your old places
because it can pull you right back into your old lifestyle.

The areas we need to discipline ourselves in are endless. *In a*
multitude of words transgression is not lacking, but he who restrains his
lips is prudent.[6] The word *prudent* means a good manager.[7] He who
restrains his words is one who doesn't say everything that comes to
his mind.

All of us have said something and then later thought, **I wish I**
had thought before I said that. Proverbs 19:11 tells us, *Good sense*
makes a man restrain his anger, and it is his glory to overlook a
transgression or an offense. That means every time someone offends
me, if I'm a wise person, I won't allow myself to become angry. I
will restrain my anger even though I may feel angry.

One of the first teaching series my brother heard as a new
believer was a series I taught on the spirit of offense. He said, "Man,
that was so good for me to hear that early in my walk with God."
He was part of our road team. Even on the road, in our teams of
fifty or so people that travel with us, they have to exercise these
principles all the time. They have to choose to not get offended.
You've got to restrain your anger.

Maybe you are too touchy. This word *restraint* doesn't make
anyone happy because people today don't want restraints. The

motto in the world today is, "If it feels good, do it!" That doesn't work; it only leads to a life of destruction. They don't want anyone telling them anything or teaching them anything. If you think that spirit is not in the church, you're wrong.

Self-control takes a decision to set your mind and keep it set. The apostle Paul had to operate in self-control. Just because he was taken up into the third heaven, doesn't mean he was never tempted. You are not an awful person because you are tempted. The question is, are you controlling the temptation?

The Bible says temptation must come. First Corinthians 9:24 says, *Do you not know that in a race all the runners compete, but [only] one receives the prize? So run [your race] that you may lay hold [of the prize] and make it yours. Now every athlete who goes into training conducts himself temperately and restricts himself in all things. . . .*

Any area of our lives can get out of balance. I don't care what it is. The Bible says, *Be well balanced (temperate, sober of mind), be vigilant and cautious at all times; for that enemy of yours, the devil, roams around like a lion roaring [in fierce hunger], seeking someone to . . . devour.*[8]

First Corinthians 9:25,26 continues, *They do it to win a wreath that will soon wither, but we [do it to receive a crown of eternal blessedness] that cannot wither. Therefore I do not run uncertainly (without definite aim). I do not box like one beating the air and striking without an adversary.* Paul is saying, "I've got a plan, and I'm working my plan. I've got a direction, and I'm sticking to my direction. I'm not just letting all these other things out here control me and cause me to lose focus."

People who cannot stay focused will never fulfill their ministry. On Monday they know what they're supposed to be doing, but they receive a phone call Monday afternoon. Someone wants to take them out to lunch and go shopping. Now all of a sudden, they can't do what they were going to do because emotions say, "Whooooo!"

Verse 27 says, *But [like a boxer] I buffet my body [handle it roughly, discipline it by hardships] and subdue it, for fear that after proclaiming to others the Gospel and things pertaining to it, I myself should become unfit [not stand the test, be unapproved and rejected as a counterfeit].*

First Corinthians 6:12 says, *Everything is permissible (allowable and lawful) for me; but not all things are helpful (good for me to do, expedient and profitable when considered with other things). Everything is lawful for me, but I will not become the slave of anything or be brought under its power.*

We're not talking about legalism. I believe many people who were undisciplined all their life will be in heaven, but not one of them will have experienced victory on earth. They missed joy and peace and will not have fulfilled the call of God on their lives. Don't let that happen to you. Make decisions to do what you know you should do, and don't quit until you have accomplished what you set out to do. Experience the joy and victory God intends for you to have on earth.

CONCLUSION

God has provided an exceptional type of life for us to live. It is manifested as we learn how to operate in the fruit of the Spirit made available to us by the grace of God. I believe teaching on the fruit of the Spirit is of great importance simply because Jesus said, "You will know them by their fruit."

Jesus wants the world to recognize those who represent Him. He wants us to give God glory as His Holy Spirit works in us and through us. He wants us to be, as His Word says, *salt*[1] and *light*.[2] Salt is supposed to make people thirsty, and light dispels the darkness. We have a very important job in God's kingdom. We are His representatives.

> *So we are Christ's ambassadors, God making His appeal*
> *as it were through us. We [as Christ's personal representatives]*
> *beg you for His sake to lay hold of the divine favor [now*
> *offered you] and be reconciled to God.*
> 2 CORINTHIANS 5:20

I challenge you to decide right now that you will live the remainder of your life striving to give glory to God in everything you do. As you make that decision and carry it out in your life, you will find your life to be exceptional beyond anything you could ever have imagined. Love, faithfulness, goodness, patience, kindness, peace, humility, joy and self-control are the elements that make our lives exceptional; they are a reward in themselves. We were born to display them, and we will never be fulfilled without them.

But seek (aim at and strive after) first of all His kingdom and
His righteousness (His way of doing and being right), and then
all these things taken together will be given you besides.
MATTHEW 6:33

PRAYER FOR A PERSONAL RELATIONSHIP WITH THE LORD

God wants you to receive His free gift of salvation. Jesus wants to save you and fill you with the Holy Spirit more than anything. If you have never invited Jesus, the Prince of Peace, to be your Lord and Savior, I invite you to do so now. Pray the following prayer, and if you are really sincere about it, you will experience a new life in Christ.

Father,

You loved the world so much, You gave Your only begotten Son to die for our sins so that whoever believes in Him will not perish, but have eternal life.

Your Word says we are saved by grace through faith as a gift from You. There is nothing we can do to earn salvation.

I believe and confess with my mouth that Jesus Christ is Your Son, the Savior of the world. I believe He died on the cross for me and bore all of my sins, paying the price for them. I believe in my heart that You raised Jesus from the dead.

I ask You to forgive my sins. I confess Jesus as my Lord. According to Your Word, I am saved and will spend eternity with You! Thank You, Father. I am so grateful! In Jesus' name, amen.

See John 3:16; Ephesians 2:8,9; Romans 10:9,10; 1 Corinthians 15:3,4; 1 John 1:9; 4:14-16; 5:1,12,13.

ENDNOTES

INTRODUCTION

1 Galatians 5:22,23.

2 1 Corinthians 12:1 AMP; see also 1 Corinthians 12:8-10.

3 See 1 Corinthians 12:1,4-7 KJV and 1 Corinthians 12:31 AMP, NKJV.

4   *Pursue love, yet desire earnestly spiritual gifts, but especially that you may prophesy* (1 Corinthians 14:1 NASB).

5   *But earnestly desire the greater gifts.*

    And I show you a still more excellent way (1 Corinthians 12:31 NASB).

6   *But earnestly desire and zealously cultivate the greatest and best gifts and graces (the higher gifts and the choicest graces). And yet I will show you a still more excellent way [one that is better by far and the highest of them all — love]* (1 Corinthians 12:31 AMP).

7 1 Corinthians 12:9 NKJV.

8 We see from the value placed on love in 1 Corinthians 13 that love is to be the basis of our actions and expression. This chapter gives several examples of gifts or attributes that we may have or actions that we may take that are meaningless without love.

The description of love's expression describes the attributes of all the fruit of the Spirit, allowing us to see that the other fruit issue from the fruit of love. All the fruit issue from God's love because God is love.

9   *. . . God is love* (1 John 4:8).

10 Matthew 12:33.

11   *Beware of false prophets, who come to you dressed as sheep, but inside they are devouring wolves.*

    You will fully recognize them by their fruits. *Do people pick grapes from thorns, or figs from thistles?*

    Even so, every healthy (sound) tree bears good fruit [worthy of admiration], but the sickly (decaying, worthless) tree bears bad (worthless) fruit.

    A good (healthy) tree cannot bear bad (worthless) fruit, nor can a bad (diseased) tree bear excellent fruit [worthy of admiration].

Every tree that does not bear good fruit is cut down and cast into the fire.

*Therefore, **you will fully know them by their fruits** (Matthew 7:15-20).*

Yes, the way to identify a tree or a person is by the kind of fruit produced (v. 20 TLB).

[12] *By this all men will know that you are my disciples, if you love one another* (John 13:35 NIV).

[13] God's love for us causes us to love Him. (See 1 John 4:19; John 3:16.) His *goodness*, or *kindness*, (fruit of the Spirit) leads us to repentance. (See Romans 2:4 KJV and NASB respectively.)

[14] See Psalm 34:8.

[15] See Proverbs 11:30.

[16] See John 10:10.

[17] *You are our letter, written in our hearts, known and read by all men; being manifested that you are a letter of Christ, cared for by us, written not with ink, but with the Spirit of the living God, not on tablets of stone, but on tablets of human hearts* (2 Corinthians 3:2,3 NASB).

[No] you yourselves are our letter of recommendation (our credentials), written in your hearts, to be known (perceived, recognized) and read by everybody.

You show and make obvious that you are a letter from Christ delivered by us, not written with ink. . . (AMP).

[18] Psalm 34:8 NKJV.

[19] See Psalm 34:8.

[20] Psalm 34:10 NKJV.

CHAPTER 1

[1] *So he said to me, "This is the word of the LORD to Zerubbabel: 'Not by might nor by power, but by my Spirit,' says the LORD Almighty"* (Zechariah 4:6 NIV). We see from the above verse that we can operate not by our own might nor power, but by the Lord's Spirit.

[2] See Ephesians 4:8; 1 Corinthians 12:1,4-11.

[3] The Bible tells us that a Christian is the temple of the living God. (See 2 Corinthians 6:16.) We need to take good care of our bodies.

CHAPTER 2

[1] See Romans 12:4-8.

[2] See 1 Corinthians 12:4-7,11.

[3] *His intention was the perfecting and the full equipping of the saints (His consecrated people), [that they should do] the work of ministering toward building up Christ's body (the church)* (Ephesians 4:12).

[4] Ephesians 4:11.

[5] See Ephesians 4:8,11-16.

[6] 1 Corinthians 12:1,4-11.

[7] 1 Corinthians 12:7 NKJV.

[8] *For the body is not one member, but many. . . .*

If the whole body were an eye, where would the hearing be? If the whole were hearing, where would the sense of smell be?

But now God has placed the members, each one of them, in the body, just as He desired.

And if they were all one member, where would the body be?

But now there are many members, but one body (1 Corinthians 12:14,17-20 NASB).

[9] See Galatians 5:19-23.

[10] See Galatians 5:25,26 NIV.

[11] See John 1:23.

[12] John 3:26.

[13] John 3:27.

[14] Romans 12:8.

[15] 1 Corinthians 12:28.

[16] See Romans 12:6-8.

[17] See Proverbs 28:20.

[18] See Psalm 75:6,7.

CHAPTER 3

1   *Now concerning spiritual gifts, brethren, I would not have you ignorant*
(1 Corinthians 12:1 KJV).

2 See 1 Corinthians 14:12 NASB.

3   *So also you, since you are zealous of spiritual gifts, seek to abound for the edification*
of the church (1 Corinthians 14:12 NASB).

   Even so you, since you are zealous for spiritual gifts, let it be for the edification of
the church that you seek to excel (NKJV).

   So it is with yourselves; since you are so eager and ambitious to possess spiritual
endowments and manifestations of the [Holy] Spirit, [concentrate on] striving to excel
and to abound [in them] in ways that will build up the church (AMP).

4 See Ephesians 4:11,12.

5 In discussing the qualifications for a leader (1 Timothy 3:1-13) — a *bishop* or an
overseer (verse 2 KJV and NIV, respectively) in this case — Paul mentions that a
novice or *recent convert* should not be selected because they may become *lifted up*
with pride or *conceited* (verse 6 KJV and NIV, respectively).

6 1 Corinthians 12:31.

7 1 Corinthians 14:1 NASB.

8   *What is the outcome then, brethren? When you assemble. . . . Let all things be done*
for edification (1 Corinthians 14:26 NASB).

   What then, brethren, is [the right course]? When you meet together. . . . let
everything be constructive and edifying and for the good of all (AMP).

9   *. . . greater is one who prophesies than one who speaks in tongues, unless he*
interprets, so that the church may receive edifying (1 Corinthians 14:5 NASB).

10   *Therefore if the whole church comes together in one place, and all speak with*
tongues, and there come in those who are uninformed or unbelievers, will they not say
that you are out of your mind?

   But if all prophesy, and an unbeliever or an uninformed person comes in, he is
convinced by all, he is convicted by all.

   And thus the secrets of his heart are revealed; and so, falling down on his face, he
will worship God and report that God is truly among you (1 Corinthians 14:23-25
NKJV).

11 *Now I wish that you all spoke in tongues, but even more that you would prophesy . . .* (1 Corinthians 14:5 NASB).

12 *I thank God, I speak in tongues more than you all* (1 Corinthians 14:18 NASB).

13 See 1 Corinthians 14:5.

14 1 Corinthians 14:4 NASB.

15 1 Corinthians 14:2 NASB.

16 KJV.

17 See AMP and NIV.

CHAPTER 4

1 1 Samuel 16:7.

2 Hebrews 10:25.

3 Genesis 1:28.

4 *Noah Webster's First Edition of an American Dictionary of the English Language,* (San   Francisco: the Foundation for American Christian Education, 1967 and 1995 by Rosalie J. Slater. Permission to reprint the 1828 edition granted by G. & C. Merriam Company), s.v. "fruitful."

5 Matthew 21:19.

6 Matthew 21:18,19.

7 *Brood of vipers! How can you, being evil, speak good things? For out of the abundance of the heart the mouth speaks.*

A good man out of the good treasure of his heart brings forth good things, and an evil man out of the evil treasure brings forth evil things (Matthew 12:34,35 NKJV).

8 2 Corinthians 5:20.

CHAPTER 5

1 See Psalm 1:1-3 AMP, NKJV.

2 1 Corinthians 12:1 KJV.

3 *Ye know that ye were Gentiles, carried away unto these dumb idols, even as ye were led.*

Wherefore I give you to understand, that no man speaking by the Spirit of God calleth Jesus accursed: and that no man can say that Jesus is the Lord, but by the Holy Ghost (1 Corinthians 12:2,3 KJV).

Therefore I want you to understand that no one speaking under the power and influence of the [Holy] Spirit of God can [ever] say, Jesus be cursed! And no one can [really] say, Jesus is [my] Lord, except by and under the power and influence of the Holy Spirit (v. 3 AMP).

You will remember that before you became Christians you went around from one idol to another, not one of which could speak a single word.

But now you are meeting people who claim to speak messages from the Spirit of God. How can you know whether they are really inspired by God or whether they are fakes? Here is the test: no one speaking by the power of the Spirit of God can curse Jesus, and no one can say, "Jesus is Lord," and really mean it, unless the Holy Spirit is helping him (vv. 2,3 TLB).

4 See Matthew 7:15-20.

5 Matthew 7:18 NKJV.

6 Matthew 24:4 KJV.

7 Matthew 24:24.

8 Matthew 24:3-6,11,23,24.

9 See Proverbs 1:20-33; 2:6; 16:16; KJV.

10 See Isaiah 28:26; Proverbs 2:10,11 KJV.

11 See 1 Kings 3:7-14 NKJV.

12 1 Corinthians 12:10 KJV, NASB respectively.

13 See 1 Corinthians 2:10.

14 In 2 Corinthians 10:4,5 we learn to . . .*refute arguments and theories and reasonings and every proud and lofty thing that sets itself up against the [true] knowledge of God . . . and to . . . lead every thought and purpose away captive into the obedience of Christ.* . . . If spend a lot of time trying to figure out things that we can't figure out instead of concentrating on keeping our thoughts in line with the Word of God, we can become confused.

15 Matthew 12:34 NKJV.

16 Proverbs 10:12.

CHAPTER 6

1 Philippians 4:7 NKJV.

2 Isaiah 9:6.

3 See 1 Peter 5:6,7 and Romans 8:28.

[4] Galatians 5:22.

[5] Psalm 1:1-3.

[6]   *Knowing that you were not redeemed with corruptible things, like silver or gold, from your aimless conduct received by tradition from your fathers, but with the precious blood of Christ, as of a lamb without blemish and without spot. . . . **having been born again, not of corruptible seed but incorruptible,** through the word of God which lives and abides forever* (1 Peter 1:18,19,23 NKJV).

[7] 1 John 1:9.

CHAPTER 7

[1] Romans 5:5 KJV.

[2] 1 Corinthians 13:2.

[3] 1 Corinthians 13:1 NASB.

[4] 1 Corinthians 13:2 NASB.

[5] See 1 John 3:18.

[6] Philippians 1:9.

[7] Philippians 1:10.

[8] Daniel 6:3.

CHAPTER 8

[1] Matthew 12:34 NKJV.

[2] See Matthew 5:13-16.

[3] See John 8:12.

[4] See 2 Corinthians 5:20.

[5] 1 Corinthians 1:9.

[6] *American Dictionary of the English Language,* 10th Ed.(San Francisco: Foundation for American Christian Education, 1998). Facsimile of Noah Webster's 1828 edition, permission to reprint by G. & C. Merriam Company, copyright 1967 & 1995 (Renewal) by Rosalie J. Slater, s.v. "FAITHFUL."

[7] *American Dictionary of the English Language,* s.v. "FAITHFULLY."

[8] Proverbs 17:17.

[9]   *If we are faithless, He remains faithful; for He cannot deny Himself* (2 Timothy 2:13 NASB).

[10] See Matthew 25:21-23.

CHAPTER 9

1   *Good and upright is the Lord; therefore will He instruct sinners in [His] way* (Psalm 25:8).

2   *Oh, how great is Your goodness, which You have laid up for those who fear, revere, and worship You, goodness which You have wrought for those who trust and take refuge in You before the sons of men!* (Psalm 31:19).

3   Psalm 31:19.

4   Psalm 23:6.

5   Exodus 33:20-23.

6   Acts 9:3-6.

7   Psalm 27:13.

8   John 14:6 KJV.

9   John 14:27 NASB.

10 Psalm 103:20.

11 *And therefore the Lord [earnestly] waits [expecting, looking, and longing] to be gracious to you. . .* (Isaiah 30:18).

12 Genesis 37:3-5.

13 See Genesis 50:20.

14 Romans 8:28 NASB.

15 Galatians 6:10.

16 1 Timothy 6:17,18.

CHAPTER 10

1   Mark 4:26-28.

2   If you would like more teaching on that subject, I have written a book by that title: *Enjoying Where You Are on the Way to Where You Are Going.*

3   See Psalm 7:9.

4   See 1 Peter 5:7.

5   Deuteronomy 8:2.

6   1 Corinthians 10:13.

7   See Romans 8:16,17; 2 Corinthians 5:17.

CHAPTER 11

1 Based on a definition from *Webster's II New College Dictionary* (Boston/New York: Houghton Mifflin Company, 1995), s.v. "mercy."

2 Brown, Driver, Briggs and Gesenius. "Hebrew Lexicon entry for Checed". *The KJV Old Testament Hebrew Lexicon*. <http://www.biblestudytools.net/Lexicons/Hebrew/heb.cgi?number=2617& version=kjv>, s.v. "kindness."

3 Matthew 5:44 NKJV.

4 1 John 4:8.

5 See Romans 2:4.

6 Romans 12:19.

7 Matthew 5:7.

8 Galatians 6:7.

9 See Mark 2:17

10 Romans 8:1.

11 1 Timothy 1:13.

12 Acts 8:3.

13 Luke 23:34 KJV.

14 Acts 7:60.

CHAPTER 12

1 Hebrews 10:12,13.

2 Philippians 4:7 NKJV.

3 1 Peter 1:8 KVJ.

4 See Genesis 8:22.

5 See Romans 12:16,18.

6 Nehemiah 8:10.

7 See Luke 10:1,5,9.

8 See 2 Corinthians 6:16.

9 Mark 4:39.

10 Deuteronomy 8:5

11 John 8:32.

[12] 2 Corinthians 5:17.

[13] Philippians 4:13.

[14] John 13:34.

CHAPTER 13

[1] 1 Samuel 15:17.

[2] See Matthew 23:27.

[3] Hebrews 11:6 KJV.

[4] 2 Corinthians 1:10.

[5] *American Dictionary of the English Language*, s.v. "HUMILITY."

[6] 1 Timothy 3:6 NKJV.

[7] Philippians 4:13 KJV.

[8] John 15:5.

[9] Luke 22:31,32.

[10] Mark 14:71.

[11] 1 Peter 5:5

[12] 1 Peter 5:6.

CHAPTER 14

[1] Based on a definition from *American Dictionary of the English Language*, s.v. "JOY."

[2] Based on a definition from *American Dictionary of the English Language*, s.v. "JOY."

[3] Based on a definition from James Strong, "Dictionary of the Words in the Greek Testament" in *Strong's Exhaustive Concordance of the Bible* (Nashville: Abingdon, 1890), p. 77, entry #5479, s.v. "joy," Galatians 5:22.

[4] Exodus 3:14.

[5] Ephesians 5:18,19 NKJV.

[6] Psalm 18:29.

[7] Deuteronomy 30:19.

[8] John 10:10.

[9] See Deuternonomy 1:29.

[10] See 2 Corinthians 5:21.

[11] 2 Corinthians 5:17.

[12] See Ecclessiastes 3:4.

[13] See Psalm 3:3.

[14] Deuteronomy 34:8.

[15] Psalm 30:5 KJV.

[16] Joel 3:14.

[17] Joshua 1:2,3.

[18] See 1 Samuel 9:15-27.

[19] See Psalm 92:10; 112:9.

CHAPTER 15

[1] 1 Corinthians 12:7

[2] John 13:34,35.

[3] 1 Corinthians 11:1.

[4] James 3:8.

[5] Galatians 6:9.

[6] Proverbs 10:19.

[7] Based on a definition from *Webster's II New College Dictionary* (Boston/New York: Houghton Mifflin Company, 1995), s.v. "prudent."

[8] 1 Peter 5:8.

CONCLUSION

[1] See Matthew 5:13.

[2] See Matthew 5:14.

ABOUT THE AUTHOR

Joyce Meyer has been teaching the Word of God since 1976 and in full-time ministry since 1980. Previously the associate pastor at Life Christian Church in St. Louis, Missouri, she developed, coordinated, and taught a weekly meeting known as "**Life In The Word.**"After more than five years, the Lord brought it to a conclusion, directing her to establish her own ministry and call it "**Life In The Word, Inc.**"

Now, her **Life In The Word** radio and television broadcasts are seen and heard by millions across the United States and throughout the world. Joyce's teaching tapes are enjoyed internationally, and she travels extensively conducting **Life In The Word** conferences.

Joyce and her husband, Dave, the business administrator at **Life In The Word,** have been married for over 35 years. They reside in St. Louis, Missouri, and are the parents of four children. All four children are married and, along with their spouses, work with Dave and Joyce in the ministry.

Believing the call on her life is to establish believers in God's Word, Joyce says, "Jesus died to set the captives free, and far too many Christians have little or no victory in their daily lives." Finding herself in the same situation many years ago and having found freedom to live in victory through applying God's Word, Joyce goes equipped to set captives free and to exchange ashes for beauty. She believes that every person who walks in victory leads many others into victory. Her life is transparent, and her teachings are practical and can be applied in everyday life.

Joyce has taught on emotional healing and related subjects in meetings all over the country, helping multiplied thousands. She has recorded more than 225 different audiocassette albums and over 100 videos. She has also authored 51 books to help the body of Christ on various topics.

Her "Emotional Healing Package" contains over 23 hours of teaching on the subject. Albums included in this package are: "Confidence"; "Beauty for Ashes" (includes Joyce's teaching notes); "Managing Your Emotions"; "Bitterness, Resentment, and Unforgiveness"; "Root of Rejection"; and a 90-minute Scripture/music tape titled "Healing the Brokenhearted."

Joyce's "Mind Package" features five different audio tape series on the subject of the mind. They include: "Mental Strongholds and Mindsets"; "Wilderness Mentality"; "The Mind of the Flesh"; "The Wandering, Wondering Mind"; and "Mind, Mouth, Moods, and Attitudes." The package also contains Joyce's powerful book, *Battlefield of the Mind*. On the subject of love she has three tape series titled "Love Is..."; "Love: The Ultimate Power"; and "Loving God, Loving Yourself, and Loving Others," and a book titled *Reduce Me to Love*.

Write to Joyce Meyer's office for a resource catalog and further information on how to obtain the tapes you need to bring total healing to your life.

To contact the author write:

Joyce Meyer Ministries
P. O. Box 655
Fenton, Missouri 63026

or call: (636) 349-0303

Internet Address: www.joycemeyer.org

Please include your testimony or help received from this book when you write. Your prayer requests are welcome.

To contact the author
in Canada, please write:

Joyce Meyer Ministries Canada, Inc.
Lambeth Box 1300
London, ON N6P 1T5

or call: (636) 349-0303

In Australia, please write:

Joyce Meyer Ministries-Australia
Locked Bag 77
Mansfield Delivery Centre
Queensland 4122

or call: 07 3349 1200

In England, please write:

Joyce Meyer Ministries
P. O. Box 1549
Windsor
SL4 1GT

or call: (0) 1753-831102

BOOKS BY JOYCE MEYER

Secrets to Exceptional Living

Eight Ways to Keep the Devil under Your Feet

Teenagers Are People Too!

Filled with the Spirit

A Celebration of Simplicity

The Joy of Believing Prayer

Never Lose Heart

Being the Person God Made You to Be

A Leader in the Making

"Good Morning, This Is God!" Gift Book

JESUS — Name Above All Names

"Good Morning, This Is God!" Daily Calendar

Help Me — I'm Married!

Reduce Me to Love

Be Healed in Jesus' Name

How to Succeed at Being Yourself

Eat and Stay Thin

Weary Warriors, Fainting Saints

Life in the Word Journal

Life in the Word Devotional

Be Anxious for Nothing

Be Anxious for Nothing Study Guide

The Help Me! Series:
I'm Alone!
I'm Stressed! • I'm Insecure!
I'm Discouraged! • I'm Depressed!
I'm Worried! • I'm Afraid!

Don't Dread

Managing Your Emotions

CPSIA information can be obtained
at www.ICGtesting.com
Printed in the USA
LVOW11*0612310117

522645LV00007B/39/P